WELCOME THE SPIRIT

*A Catechist's
Confirmation Handbook*

WELCOME THE SPIRIT

*A Catechist's
Confirmation Handbook*

Sister Mary Bernard Potter SP
and
Nigel Bavidge

GEOFFREY
CHAPMAN

Geoffrey Chapman
An imprint of Cassell Publishers Limited
Villiers House, 41–47 Strand, London WC2N 5JE
387 Park Avenue South, New York, NY 10016-8810

© Sister Mary Bernard Potter SP and Nigel Bavidge 1993

All rights reserved. This book, text and illustrations, is protected by copyright. However, pp. 11–13, 16–18, 25–30, 35–44, 50–57, 62–65, 71–76, 82–84, 91–96, 102–106, 112–115, 123–133, 137–138, and 142–147 may be photocopied or reproduced on to an overhead transparency without fee or prior permission subject to both of the following conditions: that the page is reprinted in its entirety, including the copyright acknowledgement; that the copies are used solely within the church or group that purchased the original book. For copying in all other circumstances prior written permission must be sought from the publishers.

First published 1993

ISBN 0–225–66660–X

British Library Cataloguing-in-Publication Data
A catalogue record for this book is available from the British Library.

Library of Congress Cataloging-in-Publication Data
Available from the Library of Congress.

Typeset by Fakenham Photosetting Ltd, Fakenham, Norfolk
Printed and bound in Great Britain by
Short Run Press Limited, Exeter

Contents

Foreword	vii
WELCOME TO THE PROGRAMME	1
SETTING UP THE PROGRAMME	14
COME AND SEE An introductory session for parents, candidates, catechists and priests	19
Unit 1 getting to know you	31
Unit 2 belonging	45
CELEBRATION OF ENROLMENT	58
Unit 3 sign and symbol	66
Unit 4 alive in the sacraments	77
Unit 5 gifts of the spirit	85
Unit 6 you will be my witnesses	97
CELEBRATION OF ELECTION	107
Unit 7 preparing to celebrate	116
CELEBRATION OF SENDING FORTH	134
Unit 8 into the future	139

FOREWORD

The Sacrament of Confirmation is a key moment in the life of a young Christian. It is now that the responsibilities of the following of Christ are publicly acknowledged by the individual for the first time. The sign the candidate makes is the renewal of baptismal vows. The sign the Church makes is prayer and the anointing with chrism. The Holy Spirit touches the candidate with his gifts. The moment is then sealed by the reception of the Eucharist, so completing formally the individual's full entry into the Church.

The preparation for this sacrament must be undertaken with great care, to ensure that the candidates know what they are doing, and can begin to come to terms with the way they will be expected to live as their pilgrimage continues.

I am delighted to be able to recommend to you *Welcome the Spirit*. It is a scheme of work that has grown over the years, greatly benefiting from the advice given by those catechists who have used it for their confirmation programmes. It helps candidates and catechists alike in the preparation process. It helps to involve the candidates' parents and indeed the whole parish. I hope it will encourage the parish to take some responsibility after the celebration of the sacrament for the continuing formation in faith of the young people concerned. It is an invaluable resource for parish catechists and parish clergy. I thank its authors for all that they have put into the scheme, and I wish it great success.

✠ David Konstant
Bishop of Leeds

20 March 1992

For it is not ourselves that we are preaching, but Christ Jesus as the Lord, and ourselves as servants for Jesus' sake. It is the same God who said 'Let there be light shining out of darkness', who has shone in our minds to radiate the light of the knowledge of God's glory, the glory on the face of Christ.

We are only the earthenware jars that hold this treasure, to make it clear that such an overwhelming power comes from God and not from us.

2 Corinthians 4:5–7

WELCOME TO THE PROGRAMME

Welcome to this Confirmation Preparation Programme which has been designed for use with young people aged 13-plus.

Welcome the Spirit has been written with you, the busy priest, and you, the busy catechist, in mind.

The programme contains detailed guidance and content for preparing young people, aged 13 to 16 years old, for the Sacrament of Confirmation.

There are also

- activity sheets
- letters
- celebration sheets

all of which can be photocopied and which we hope will make life a lot easier for you.

The material, based on the structure of the Rite of Christian Initiation of Adults (RCIA), has been organized into eight units with enough content in each for a session lasting an hour and a half. The unit content has been given in some detail but you should feel free to adapt the material so that you can make it your own.

Making the material personal is vital since it is you who must breathe life, excitement, joy and enthusiasm into these printed words.

We suggest, however, that you keep quite closely to the text when using the material for the first time, but keep a careful note of your comments and observations which can then be used as a basis for future planning and adaptation.

The purpose of parish-based sacramental programmes is to complement the work of religious education which takes place in the other two great centres of faith formation, the home and the school. This Confirmation Programme is not meant to replace the work of the home or the school, but to support it and enrich it.

Preparing young people for the sacraments through parish-based programmes adds the vital dimension to the ministry of the home and school by developing a sense of belonging to a community of faith which should remain a significant part of life when school has finished and when the young people have grown into the independence of adulthood.

Through baptism we have been called by God to a relationship which is expressed through active involvement in the worship, values and life of the Church, and which is lived out in the context of the parish community. Each parish, therefore, has the responsibility of making its young members feel welcomed, wanted and valued. Every parish has the duty of sharing its beliefs, its values and its life with them.

Parish-based preparation for the sacraments is an expression of the parish's commitment to its young people. By drawing them more deeply into the life of the community, catechists can help young people to form a solid foundation on which a lifelong faith can be built.

Welcome the Spirit

Ultimately, of course, it is the young people themselves who must make the commitment to God through the Church and this is dependent on their personal response to the gifts of God. Priests, parents, teachers and catechists cannot make this happen – the gift of faith is not yours to give – but you can provide a setting of love, openness and security in which the young people might be more receptive to the action of God's Holy Spirit.

We hope that *Welcome the Spirit* will help you to share with young people, not simply information about Confirmation, but the joy and the challenge of the Good News, so that they may be truly ready for the wonderful gift of the Spirit which is promised to them.

We are grateful for the support and encouragement of the Leeds Diocesan Religious Education Team, and the many priests and catechists who have shared with us their wide experience and insights as we prepared this programme.

CONFIRMATION AND THE PRIEST

While the catechists will be responsible for organizing and leading the sessions with the young people, the priest has a vital role to play in the preparation for Confirmation.

- It is the duty and responsibility of the priest to select and commission the catechists, ensuring that they have an adequate training.
- The priest should be a source of encouragement and support for the catechists, available to offer them advice and guidance.
- The priest will make it his concern that the catechists also develop spiritually so that they may be effective witnesses to the young people.
- While the priest may not be present for the whole of every session, he will make regular contact with the candidates during their preparation.
- Home visiting of the candidates and their families will no doubt be seen as an important part of the programme.
- Together with the catechists, the priest will be responsible for discerning the readiness of the candidates for the Sacrament.
- Through the homilies, prayers of the faithful and announcements the priest has the possibility of developing the parish's awareness of its responsibilities to the young people.
- By presiding at the various celebrations the priest will draw the young people more deeply into prayer and into the sacramental life of the parish.

Effective parish catechesis is only possible with the active encouragement, support and guidance of the priest who holds the ultimate responsibility for the spiritual growth and welfare of those in his care.

CONFIRMATION AND THE CATECHIST

As a catechist you have a very important role to play in the religious formation of young people. You bring with you so many experiences which can enrich their lives and help them to open themselves to receive the gift of the Sacrament of Confirmation.

Your enthusiasm and commitment will:

- help them to understand more deeply the meaning of the Sacrament
- encourage them to pray
- strengthen their sense of belonging to the parish community
- show them the concern and care of the parish.

Working with young people is challenging and demanding, but it is also very exciting and rewarding. As you work with them you will find that you have much to offer them and that they also have much to offer you. As you journey with them towards Confirmation you will find the need to explore and examine your own faith more closely. You may not have the answers to all of their questions, but what they need is someone willing to share the search with them. Often what young people need is someone who will listen with openness, acceptance and humour, rather than someone who knows it all!

Above all, your role is to be a friend to the candidates as they grow in their own unique relationship with God. While you will share with them the teaching element in the programme, it is who you are, rather than what you say, which will leave a lasting impression on those with whom you are sharing your faith.

CONFIRMATION AND THE CANDIDATE

As Confirmation catechists you are offering your time and energy to the young people who wish to be confirmed. It is easy to forget that just as demands are made on your time and energy, so demands are made on the candidates. They too have volunteered to be part of the preparation programme. Their willingness to give time despite other attractions and commitments should be recognized. It is, therefore, very important that the candidates should feel welcomed and valued and that enjoyment should be a key part of the meetings.

As baptized members of the Church, the young people have insights and experiences which can be of tremendous value. It is vital that the candidates know that their ideas and contributions are listened to and respected. Catechists are faith sharers and to share means to receive as well as to give. A mark of fruitful catechesis is when catechists realize that they have been enriched by those with whom they have been working.

By the age of 13, young people are developing a strong sense of their own autonomy. While they are not yet ready to be entirely independent, it is important to help them to arrive at a truly personal decision to receive the Sacrament of Confirmation, regardless of peer or parental pressure, local or parish custom. This will require great sensitivity on the part of the priests and catechists.

The beginning of the teenage years often marks the beginning of a time of questioning and doubt. Teenagers have many questions as they struggle to make sense of all they have learnt. Challenge and confrontation are often the hallmark of the teenager. Catechists must recognize this and accept that they might well be challenged by the young people. Should this happen it would be counterproductive to try to ignore it or suppress it by an exercise of adult power. If we listen respectfully to their searchings and try to identify with them, there is a much greater chance that a resolution will be found.

Teenagers can live with their questions provided that they know they are accepted and respected.

Welcome the Spirit

CONFIRMATION AND THE HOME

The home is the cradle of the faith.

Many young people have received wonderful example and teaching from their parents over the years. Their parents have been actively involved in their religious growth, responding generously to the invitation and challenge of the promises they made when their child was baptized. It is a great privilege for catechists to be allowed to share in this and offer to families support, encouragement and enrichment.

Catechists should, however, always remember that parents are the principal educators of their children in the ways of faith. While it is important that the developing independence of the young people with whom catechists are working is respected, it should not be forgotten that the home is still the most significant 'school of faith'.

Every effort should be made to:

- affirm parents for all the good work they have done,
- make parents feel involved in the Confirmation Preparation Programme by inviting them to the Introductory Session and making sure that they are invited to the Celebrations,
- ensure that parents are kept properly informed about the way the programme is organized and conducted.

For other young people there has been little support or encouragement to take part in active church life. However, we must be careful not to judge or condemn. We must be convinced that God is at work, in God's own way, within each member of every family, remembering that God's desire to share love and the sacraments with those called to Baptism is infinitely greater than ours.

The Confirmation Preparation Programme offers an opportunity to parents to re-examine their role in the faith development of their son or daughter and, by making them feel welcomed and involved, we may encourage them to discover a new enthusiasm and a new commitment to God through the life of the Church.

CONFIRMATION AND THE PARISH

Now you together make up Christ's body.
ST PAUL

Among the major developments in the Church over the last few decades has been the re-emphasis given to the teaching about the Church as a *community of faith* which is, in a special way, a visible sign of the *presence of the living Lord* among us. To be a Catholic is a call to *know and love God in and through the family of the Church*.

The parish is the pre-eminent place of catechesis.
POPE JOHN PAUL II

As a community of faith the parish has among its most important responsibilities the privilege and duty of drawing its children and young people more deeply into the life of faith. Parish-based sacramental preparation is one of the ways in which the parish can fulfil this sacred duty. These programmes aim, not only to give young people information to help them understand the sacraments, but also to help them develop a sense of belonging to the parish and an opportunity to become more actively involved in its life.

Parish-based sacramental programmes can help parishioners to heighten their awareness of the responsibility to share their faith. While the catechists act on behalf of the whole parish, every parishioner has a role to play through:

- prayer and fasting
- extending a welcome to children and young people
- showing an interest in their faith growth
- sharing in the liturgies which form part of the programme.

Here are some ideas for involving parishioners:

Prayer sponsors – Invite older members of the parish, especially those confined to their homes, to 'adopt' one of the Confirmation candidates in prayer. When the candidates have been enrolled distribute prayer cards to the prayer sponsors. (You could use the example on the handout on p. 12.)

Display – After the Enrolment Celebration, photographs and the names of the candidates and catechists can be displayed in some suitable place in the parish church.

Prayers of the Faithful – Special prayers should be included in the Prayers of the Faithful at Mass, especially as Confirmation Day draws near. If there are not too many candidates, it may be possible to pray for them by name.

Liturgies – In the Preparation Programme there are two special liturgies (the Enrolment Celebration and the Celebration of Election). When these take place, copies of the text should be available for every member of the congregation so that all can take an active part in the liturgy.

Homilies – Throughout the period of preparation reference to the Sacrament of Confirmation and the preparation for it should be included in the homily where it is appropriate.

Penance – Parishioners should be encouraged to offer their acts of penance for the Confirmation candidates. Jesus told us that our penance could help others in their struggle against evil: 'There are some things that are only untied through prayer and fasting.' Not only will this help the Confirmation candidates, it can also help parishioners to rediscover this often neglected virtue.

Bible sponsors – Our spiritual life is based on the two great pillars of the sacraments and the scriptures. Sadly many of our families do not own a copy of the Bible. The Preparation Programme provides an opportunity for presenting the candidates with Bibles. Parishioners can be invited to donate the cost of a Bible.

Parish organizations – As the young people of the community prepare for Confirmation, which calls them to a life of service and mission, it is important that parish organizations reflect on the ways in which they may offer the possibility for young people to be involved in their work.

Confirmation and the School

In a full process of religious education and formation, there are a number of specific activities which take place. These are:

Evangelization – the initial proclamation of the Gospel which calls us to respond in faith. In a very special way, this is the work of the *home*.

Religious education – the systematic study of religion and religious beliefs. This work is principally undertaken by *schools*.

Catechesis – the sharing of faith between believers. It aims to help them deepen their faith, committing themselves more deeply to God. Within the community of the Church, the *parish* is the most important centre for catechesis.

Obviously there is a great deal of overlap between these three activities. In schools, evangelization and catechesis will take place, but, even though that is true, religious education remains its principal activity. Parish-based sacramental programmes also allow for these three activities, but catechesis is the main one.

Even though there is overlap between the activities and the places where these activities take place, it is important to remember that sacramental programmes are not a substitute for the systematic religious education offered in schools. The principal aim of a parish-based programme is to allow for faith sharing leading to a deepening of faith in both the candidates for Confirmation and in the catechists.

It is therefore important to remember:

- there will be gaps in the candidates' knowledge since their formal religious eduction is not yet complete. Don't be surprised when you discover these gaps and resist the temptation to try to fill them all. Respond only to those which are essential to the Confirmation Preparation.
- that the Confirmation Preparation Programme does not aim to convey everything to be taught or learnt about the Sacrament. Be confident that the candidates have a lifetime in which to learn and discover more. Teenagers can only learn in a teenage way. We cannot expect them to have an adult appreciation of what will always be mystery. Allow the Holy Spirit to work.
- that parish-based preparation is distinct from formal school education. The style of the sessions should be very different from a formal classroom lesson. Avoid using terms or words like 'Confirmation class', 'pupils', 'homework', etc. Remember you are principally involved with these young people as a faith sharer and fellow parishioner. The complex skills required for formal education are quite different from those of a parish catechist.

> The school continues to be an essential part of the Church's teaching ministry. Its principal role is to support the work of the home and the parish in deepening the child's religious education. Therefore, regardless of when and how a child is presented for Confirmation, the school will provide a continuing programme of sacramental education. The school, however, cannot and should not be expected to substitute for the first two basic communities, the home and the parish.
> *Leeds Diocesan Guidelines on Confirmation*

CONFIRMATION AND CELEBRATION

Welcome to the Programme

Prayer forms one of the essential elements of any catechesis and, in this Confirmation Programme, suggestions for prayer and celebration have been included as an intrinsic part of the process. In every Unit there is a fundamental catechetical process at work.

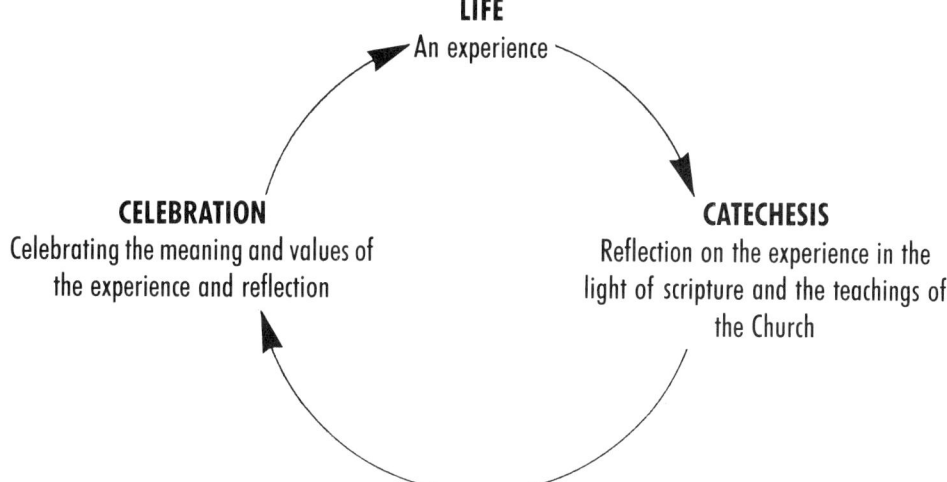

It is by following this process that life and religion become inextricably bound and come to be understood as interrelated. The importance of effective and meaningful prayer and liturgical celebration cannot be overestimated. It is through them that:

- we open ourselves to God's gifts through adoration, praise, thanksgiving, contrition and petition
- we joyfully recognize God's action in our lives
- we find strength to deal with life's difficulties
- we become aware of the sacredness of all things
- we develop our sense of community
- we strengthen our community bonds
- we celebrate what we hold to be true and what we value
- we deepen our commitment to those truths and values.

Good liturgy and community prayers, through their signs and symbols, speak to us at levels which go beyond words and teaching. They are capable of touching the heart in ways in which no other activity in religious formation is able. They have the power to lead to conversion of heart.

It is, therefore, very important that the liturgies and prayer times experienced by the young people throughout the course of the Confirmation Preparation Programme should be of the highest quality. While suggested formats have been offered in the text, catechists should feel free to adapt the ideas or replace them so that they are able to lead the prayer from the heart and convey a deep sense of personal commitment.

When praying with young people it is useful to bear the following points in mind:

- it is a myth that young people only enjoy boisterous activity. Silence, the beginning of openness, is very often enjoyed and valued by young people. Some, however, may need time to learn how to enter into stillness and silence. You may find it helpful to teach them some of the relaxation techniques which are now quite well known.

- quiet, unobtrusive taped music can help to support young people as they learn how to be silent. It can also help in creating a prayerful atmosphere.
- before beginning a formal prayer time, it is always advisable to have some period of quietness.
- when there is a reading from scripture, it is better to use the book of the Bible rather than a printed sheet. Even if this is not possible (for example, when the reading consists of a selection of verses from a chapter) a Bible should be placed in a prominent position and its importance highlighted by placing a candle and flowers beside it.

The formal liturgies leading up to the Sacramental Celebration, namely:

> the Celebration of Enrolment
> the Celebration of Election
> the Celebration of Sending Forth

form an important part of the programme. These liturgies, which are based on the process underpinning the Rite of Christian Initiation of Adults, are designed to:

- highlight for the young people the seriousness of the sacraments of the Church
- enrich their liturgical experience
- make the whole parish more aware of the sacraments as gifts to the whole community.

Suggested texts for the celebrations (except the Rite of Confirmation) are given but they can be adapted. When preparing the celebrations, including the Rite of Confirmation, it is important to:

- involve the candidates in preparing the celebration
- where choices are offered (e.g. in the choice of readings, hymns, etc.) candidates should be consulted
- if possible candidates should be involved in writing the Prayers of the Faithful
- the candidates should be involved in the Presentation of the Gifts, readings, Prayers of the Faithful.

While the celebrations are celebrations of the whole community, the young people should feel that in a very special way they belong to them.

CONFIRMATION AND THE RETREAT

Why a residential retreat?

One of the most valuable opportunities for religious formation which can be offered to young people preparing for Confirmation is the residential retreat. Experience shows that in this setting young people open themselves up to prayer, the sacraments and sharing deep concerns in ways which can rarely be achieved elsewhere.

It is strongly recommended that, if at all possible, a residential retreat should be part of the Confirmation Preparation Programme.

A residential retreat has four purposes:

- it develops a deep sense of community among all the participants, candidates and catechists, which in turn helps to deepen the sense of belonging to the parish.

- it provides opportunities for a wide and different experience of entering into relationship with God through prayer.
- it allows for personal and intimate experiences of liturgy and sacramental celebration.
- it is designed to create space, away from everyday life, in order to reflect on God's call and ways of responding to it. For many it becomes an experience of conversion.

The place of the residential retreat in the Preparation Programme

This Confirmation Preparation Programme has been constructed following the model of the Rite of Christian Initiation of Adults (RCIA). The retreat corresponds to the Period of Enlightenment which follows the Rite of Election. This period is the immediate preparation for the Celebration of the Sacrament and so is concerned with prayer and reconciliation.

Ideally, therefore, the residential retreat should take place after the Celebration of Election. This may not always be possible. If it is not, the residential retreat should take place as near to the Celebration of Election as possible.

Organizing and involving young people over an extended period of time in a residential retreat demands very special skills. It is recommended that the expertise of experienced retreat givers should be used. Their involvement adds a new, rich and varied dimension to the young people's formation. The catechists, however, even when outside expertise is being used, have an important role to play in the retreat. Apart from supervising the young people, the retreat offers them the opportunity to share as equals in the activities, prayer and liturgies. Thus they witness to their own faith and deepen their relationships with the young people.

Catechists should regard involvement in the retreat as an intrinsic part of their commitment and ministry.

Content of the residential retreat

Because every group is different, it is impossible to outline in any detail the content of the retreat. However, it is suggested that the overall theme should be: The Spirit of Peace.

This will allow for an exploration of peace at many different levels, e.g. peace in the world, peace at home, peace in our hearts, and will, therefore, lead naturally into a consideration and celebration of the Sacrament of Reconciliation.

In preparing for the retreat a careful briefing session should take place involving the catechists, who know the young people, and the retreat leader or team. In this way it can be ensured that the retreat flows naturally from the parish-based sessions.

Organization of the residential retreat

- Because of the heavy demand on retreat centres it will be necessary to book the retreat as soon as possible (most centres are booked at least a year in advance).
- A planning session with the retreat leader or team should be built into the total planning of the programme.
- If at all possible all the catechists should take part in the retreat. It is a legal

requirement that if girls are in residence there must be an adult woman with them. It is advisable to have no less than one catechist to ten candidates.

- While it may not be possible for the priest to be away from the parish for the whole of the retreat, he should spend as much time as possible with his young parishioners.

- The parish priest and his finance commission should consider the funding of the retreat as a legitimate parish expenditure, though families should be invited to make a contribution.

- As a safeguard it is important that a parent or guardian of each young person on the retreat should sign a consent form. A suggested format is the handout on p. 13.

A retreat day

While a residential retreat is the ideal, it may not be always possible to organize such an event. In that case a retreat day should be organized using either parish premises or a retreat centre. The content and organization of the day should be based on the suggestions given above.

CONFIRMATION AND THE FUTURE

Throughout the course of the preparation reference is made to the fact that Confirmation is a call to mission.

For most people this mission is lived out in the ordinary and everyday events of life at home, at work, in the neighbourhood and in the parish. It does, however, take a great deal of maturity to understand that our Christian service is concerned with making holy every moment of our lives.

Young people need opportunities to develop their sense of mission and service. Having been challenged throughout their preparation for Confirmation it is essential that the parish community provides the opportunities for service which will use the energy and enthusiasm of the young people.

Thought ought to be given to establishing service projects or organizations, such as Junior SVP, Junior Legion, Junior Third World Group, Junior Gospel Study/Prayer Group or YCW. Unless such opportunities are available we cannot be surprised if the catechesis about mission does not move into action.

Whatever is made available for young people must be organized and directed by them. Adult guidance and support will be necessary, but should always be unobtrusive, recognizing the desire of young people to take personal responsibility.

Whatever you ask
in my name
will be given to you

Please pray for

_____

who is preparing to receive
the Sacrament of Confirmation

on _____

© Sister Mary Bernard Potter SP and Nigel Bavidge 1993.
Multiple copies of these pages may be made by the purchasing church or group only.

Father,
pour out your Spirit
upon your people,
especially on

who is preparing to receive the
Sacrament of Confirmation,
and grant us all
a new vision of your glory,
a new experience of your power,
a new faithfulness to your work,
a new consecration to your service,
that your love may grow among us,
and your kingdom come;
through Christ, our Lord.
Amen.

Holy Spirit come in power to

and fill him with your love,
your strength and your peace.
May he become a loyal follower
of Jesus, our Lord,
and a witness to his
message of love
for the world.

Glory be to the Father and to the Son
and to the Holy Spirit,
as it was in the beginning,
is now, and ever shall be,
world without end.
Amen.

Father,
pour out your Spirit
upon your people,
especially on

who is preparing to receive the
Sacrament of Confirmation,
and grant us all
a new vision of your glory,
a new experience of your power,
a new faithfulness to your work,
a new consecration to your service,
that your love may grow among us,
and your kingdom come;
through Christ, our Lord.
Amen.

Holy Spirit come in power to

and fill her with your love,
your strength and your peace.
May she become a loyal follower
of Jesus, our Lord,
and a witness to his
message of love
for the world.

Glory be to the Father and to the Son
and to the Holy Spirit,
as it was in the beginning,
is now, and ever shall be,
world without end.
Amen.

(Parish Name
and Address)

STATEMENT OF PARENTAL CONSENT

To be completed by the parent/guardian of one who has not yet reached the age of majority.

I, _____, being the parent/guardian

of _____, give permission for him/her

to take part in the parish residential retreat at _____

_____

under the direction of _____

I also give my consent for my son/daughter to be taken for medical treatment,

should the need arise, and for the above named leaders to sign on my behalf.

Signed _____

Dated _____

- -

Please give the name, address and, very importantly, the telephone number of someone who can be contacted immediately should the need arise.

Name _____

Address _____

_____

_____

Telephone number _____

Relationship to candidate _____

© Sister Mary Bernard Potter SP and Nigel Bavidge 1993.
Multiple copies of this page may be made by the purchasing church or group only.

SETTING UP THE PROGRAMME

COUNTDOWN TO CONFIRMATION

A chart to assist with the planning is given on the handout on p. 16.

Stage one: long-term preparation (at least one year in advance)

- Establish date of Confirmation at least one year in advance
- Book date for residential retreat/retreat day
- Recruit and commence training of catechists
- Plan dates with catechists
- Issue the invitation to the Introductory Session at least one month before the planned date. (A suggested format for the invitation is given in the handout on pp. 17–18, 'Come and See'.)

Stage two (at least six months in advance)

- 'Come and See' introductory session with parents, candidates, catechists and priests.
  As the preparation begins it would be a good idea to arrange some social event, e.g. trip to ice-rink, barbecue, etc., to help the candidates and catechists to get to know each other and to develop friendships.
- Commence candidates' preparation—Unit One, Unit Two
- Enrolment Celebration
- Continue candidates' preparation—Unit Three, Unit Four, Unit Five, Unit Six
- Election Celebration
- Residential retreat/retreat day
- Continue candidates' preparation—Unit Seven
- Celebration of Sending Forth
- Celebration of the Sacrament of Confirmation.

Stage three (within one month of Confirmation)

- Conclude the programme—Unit Eight
- Catechists' evaluation and celebration.

Recommended Reading

Catechesis in Our Time, Pope John Paul II, CTS.
General Catechetical Directory, Sacred Congregation for the Clergy, CTS.
Sharing the Gift, Paddy Rylands, Collins.
Our Schools and Our Faith, Jim Gallagher, Collins.
Our Faith Story, A. Patrick Purnell, Collins.
The Ministry of Evangelization, Susan Blum, The Liturgical Press.
RCIA: A Study Book, St Thomas More Centre.
Confirmation: The Rite, CTS.
Book of Sacramental Basics, Tad Guzie, Paulist Press.
A New Look at the Sacraments, William J. Bausch, 23rd Publications.
This is Our Faith, Michael Pennock, Ave Maria Press.
Come Holy Spirit, Nigel Bavidge, Kevin Mayhew Ltd.
The Sacraments and You, Michael Pennock, Ave Maria Press.
The Pope in Britain, CTS.
Gift of Community, Thomas Marsh, Michael Glazier Inc.

SETTING UP THE PROGRAMME

PLANNER

Remember to take into consideration school holidays (don't forget half terms).

EVENT	DATE	TIME	PLACE
Catechists' Training			
Come and See (Parents, Candidates, Catechists, Priest)			
Unit One			
Unit Two			
Celebration of Enrolment			
Unit Three			
Unit Four			
Unit Five			
Unit Six			
Celebration of Election			
Retreat			
Unit Seven			
Celebration of Sending Forth			
Celebration of Sacrament of Confirmation			
Unit Eight			
Catechists' Evaluation and Celebration			

© Sister Mary Bernard Potter sp and Nigel Bavidge 1993.
Multiple copies of this page may be made by the purchasing church or group only.

Come and See

An Invitation to Confirmation

© Sister Mary Bernard Potter sp and Nigel Bavidge 1993.
Multiple copies of these pages may be made by the purchasing church or group only.

FIRST INFORMATION

The Bishop will soon be visiting our parish to celebrate the Sacrament of Confirmation. This wonderful Sacrament fulfils the promise which Jesus made on the night before he died, when he said:

> I will ask the Father to send another Advocate, who will be with you for ever.
>
> *(John 14:16)*

This helper, the Holy Spirit, gives us the strength, the courage and the love to live as Jesus taught us, and so find the peace and the joy which God alone can give.

In the name of Jesus, our parish extends an invitation to any young person, aged thirteen or older, who wishes to be confirmed with the gift of the Spirit, to share in our Parish Preparation for Confirmation.

An information evening for those young people and their families will be held:

on _____

at _____

from _____ to _____

We look forward to welcoming you at this very important meeting.

Yours sincerely,

_____ Parish Priest

If you are interested in knowing more about the Parish Confirmation Preparation please complete this form and return it to your priest as soon as possible.

Name of Candidate _____

Address _____ Telephone no. _____

Date of Birth _____

Place of Baptism
Name of Parish _____

Town of Parish _____

Date of Baptism _____

Place of First Communion
Name of Parish _____

Town of Parish _____

Date of First Communion _____

COME AND SEE

*An introductory session for parents,
candidates, catechists and priests*

SESSION AIMS

1. To give information about the Confirmation Preparation Programme.
2. To explain the roles and involvement of parents, sponsors and candidates.
3. To offer the invitation to prospective candidates to take part in the Confirmation Preparation.

OUTLINE

1. Arrivals and refreshments ⎫
2. Welcome ⎬ (*15 mins*)
3. Opening prayer ⎭
4. Introductions (*10 mins*)
5. Presentation (*15 mins*)
6. Break (*5 mins*)
7. Practical details (*30 mins*)
8. Questions (*5 mins*)
9. Prayer ⎫
10. Conclusion ⎬ (*10 mins*)

MATERIALS

'The Pope Speaks' (*handout on p. 25*)
'Practical Details' (*handout on p. 26*)
'Sponsors' (*handout on pp. 27–28*)

Documents:
  'Request for Enrolment' (*handout on p. 29*)
  'Parent Promise' (*handout on p. 30*)
Tape recorder and music
Extra copies of 'Come and See' (*handout on pp. 17–18*)

page 19

Welcome the Spirit

PREPARATION

- Refreshments—tea, coffee, juice, biscuits.
- Prepare the prayer focal point, e.g. table covered with red/white cloth on which is placed the open Bible, an attractive and reasonably sized candle and a plant or flower arrangement.
- Prepare the room: chairs grouped in circles.
- Make sure the tape is set correctly.

SESSION

1. Arrivals and refreshments

- Ensure that everyone is welcomed as they arrive (two or three members of the team ought to have specific responsibility for this).
- Tea, coffee, fruit juice and biscuits should be available.
- Allow people to mingle for a short while.

2. Welcome

- The priest and/or the chief catechist should welcome everyone (candidates, parents, catechists, helpers) to the meeting.

3. Opening prayer

- Explain that this prayer will be used to begin each of the meetings.
- Lead into the prayer using an introduction along these lines:

    God, you are father and mother to us all, we turn to you in prayer as we say ... pour out ...

(Remember that there are many titles of God, which point to different aspects of the mystery of God, e.g. Creator, Life-giver, Father, Mother, All-powerful, God of love, of life, of mercy, of power, etc. By using different ways of addressing God you can help people to be more aware of the infinite nature of God.)

> **... pour out your Spirit**
> **upon your people,**
> **and grant us**
> **a new vision of your glory,**
> **a new experience of your power,**
> **a new faithfulness to your Word,**
> **a new consecration to your service,**
> **that your love may grow among us,**
> **and your kingdom come;**
> **through Christ, our Lord.**
> **Amen.**

4. Introductions

- The Team:
  members of the team should introduce themselves, giving their names (clearly!) and one or two sentences about themselves.
- The Group:
  if the chairs are not already grouped, ask everyone to organize themselves into circles of no more than eight. Try to ensure that there is a mix of candidates, parents and catechists.

  Explain the activity *The Name Game*, i.e. the first person says: 'I am A.'; the second person says: 'I am B., and this is A. (first person)'; third person says: 'I am C., and this is B. (second person) and this is A. (first person)'; and so on round the circle.

5. Presentation

- The priest or one of the catechists should give a short presentation (lasting no more than 15 minutes) on the meaning of the Sacrament of Confirmation. It may be useful to use, as a structure for this, the handout on p. 25, 'The Pope Speaks'.
- Some pointers are given here, but it is essential that whoever gives the presentation makes these ideas their own, presenting them with a deep sense of commitment and enthusiasm.

  > **Christ's gift of the Holy Spirit is going to be poured out upon you in a particular way.**

- The Holy Spirit already dwells in us through Baptism, but in Confirmation the Spirit is given to us in a new and powerful way, enabling us to become witnesses for Christ.

  > **You will hear the words of the Church spoken over you calling upon the Holy Spirit**
  > — **to confirm your faith,**
  > — **to seal you in his love,**
  > — **to strengthen you for his service.**

- The sacraments have been entrusted by Christ to the Church. While the love of God is available to all, it is through the Church's sacraments we are guaranteed the fullness of the gifts which Jesus gave us.
  — In Baptism we were chosen as God's own.
  — In Confirmation God's choice is sealed. It is therefore to be seen as a completion of our Baptism. God's choice is a call to bring the Gospel message into the world.

  > **You will then take your place among fellow Christians throughout the world, full citizens now of the People of God.**
  > — **You will witness to the truth of the Gospel in the name of Jesus Christ.**
  > — **You will live your lives in such a way as to make holy all human life.**
  > — **Together with all the confirmed you are called by God to be instruments of peace.**

- Confirmation makes us full members of the Church (People of God) and we therefore share in the privileges and responsibilities of the Church. We must proclaim the Gospel in our ordinary everyday lives, which is how we make all things holy.

> **The Holy Spirit comes to you in the Sacrament of Confirmation**
> — **to involve you more completely in the Church's fight against sin,**
> — **to join in her mission of fostering holiness,**
> — **to strengthen you for the struggle with evil.**

- God calls us to become fully human and to live in love and peace, but the power of evil is a real power seeking to destroy our relationships with God and with each other. We need the strength of the Spirit to overcome the destructive power of evil.

> **You will receive the gift of the Holy Spirit that you may help to bring to the world the fruits of reconciliation and peace. Strengthened by the Holy Spirit and his manifold gifts**
> — **commit yourselves wholeheartedly to the Church's struggle against sin,**
> — **strive to be unselfish,**
> — **try not to be obsessed with material things,**
> — **be active members of the People of God,**
> — **be reconciled with each other,**
> — **be devoted to the work of justice which will bring peace on earth.**

- The Holy Spirit brings to us all the gifts which are necessary for our mission. If we are to open our hearts to receive what God is offering we must enter into the struggle wholeheartedly and strive to become active and committed to the life of the Church. If we do this our world will be transformed.

> **Young people, the world of today needs you for it needs men and women who are filled with the Holy Spirit. It needs your courage and hopefulness, your faith and your perseverance. The world of tomorrow will be built by you.**

- Our young people have many gifts to bring to the Church and to the world. The future of the world is in their hands as well as in ours. In a world of greed, violence and hatred these young people need our wholehearted support and the gifts of the Holy Spirit which are being offered by God through the Church.

- This is the invitation which God is offering through our parish community. Parents have a very important part to play in this.

- At Baptism you parents promised to bring your child up to know God as members of the Church. Even though it is the young people themselves who must decide to ask for Confirmation they need your support, encouragement and example.

6. Short break

7. Practical details

Dates and times

One of the catechists should explain the reasoning behind the outline of the programme. Items to be included:

— Date of Confirmation
— Place of Confirmation
— Number of sessions for candidates and catechists
— Date and place of retreat

— Date and place of Enrolment and Election Celebrations for candidates and their families
— Date and place of candidates' next meeting.

All this information should be given on the handout on p. 26, 'Practical Details'.

Explanation of documents

Request for Enrolment—linking with the earlier Presentation (see No. 5 above), one of the catechists should introduce the handout on p. 29, the 'Request for Enrolment' document.

It should be stressed that:
(a) this is *an invitation*
(b) the candidate must freely choose to complete the document.

Parent Promise—again, making the links, the handout on p. 30, the 'Parent Promise' document, should be explained by one of the catechists.

It should be stressed that:
(a) these documents should be signed at home only after family discussion, reflection and prayer;
(b) these documents will be required for the Celebration of Enrolment.

Choosing a sponsor

Distribute the handout on pp. 27–28, 'Sponsors', and go through it.

Candidate's files

Ask parents to provide an A4 folder for the candidates' use at the sessions.

8. Questions

Allow a short time for questions.

9. Prayer

- Invite everyone to arrange their chairs in a semicircle ready for the prayer time.
- Begin by playing a piece of quiet music (e.g. Taizé *'Veni, Sancte Spiritus'*) then, over the music, say the following invitation to prayer, or compose one:

  Let us be still and know that God is with us ...
  Let us put before our God all that we have shared this evening ...
  God invites us, through Jesus, to grow in faith and love ...
  Let us listen to the Word of our God.

(let music fade away)

Reading (John 1:35–39)

A reading from St John's Gospel.
> John was standing with two of his disciples when he saw Jesus walking by.
> 'There is the Lamb of God!' he said.
> The two disciples heard him say this and went with Jesus.
> Jesus turned, saw them following him, and asked:
> 'What are you looking for?'
> They answered:
> 'Where do you live, Rabbi?' (This word means teacher.)
> 'Come and see', he answered.
> So they went with him and saw where he lived and spent the rest of the day with him.

This is the Word of our God.

> **Let us pray:**
> **Lord Jesus,**
> **we thank you for your invitation**
> **to come and see where you live in our lives.**
> **Give us open hearts**
> **so that we might generously accept your call**
> **to live, through the power of your Spirit,**
> **as children of God.**
> **Amen.**

10. Conclusion

- Remember to thank everyone for coming to the meeting.
- One of the catechists reminds the group of the date, time and place of the next meeting of the candidates and catechists.
- Any family with individual questions is invited to contact the priest or one of the catechists after the meeting.
- Ensure that every prospective candidate has completed the 'First Information' form on the handout on pp. 17–18, 'Come and See'. (Copies should be available for any who have not already handed in the form.)

Team reflection

1. Did the session go well? Make a note of any adaptations you would recommend for future use.
2. Have any problems emerged? How can they be dealt with?

COME AND SEE

THE POPE SPEAKS

'Christ's gift of the Holy Spirit is going to be poured out upon you in a particular way.'

'You will hear the words of the Church spoken over you calling upon the Holy Spirit:
- to confirm your faith,
- to seal you in his love,
- to strengthen you for his service.'

'You will then take your place among fellow Christians throughout the world, full citizens now of the People of God.
- You will witness to the truth of the Gospel in the name of Jesus Christ.
- You will live your lives in such a way as to make holy all human life.
- Together with all the confirmed you are called by God to be instruments of his peace.'

'The Holy Spirit comes to you in the Sacrament of Confirmation
- to involve you more completely in the Church's fight against sin;
- to join in her mission of fostering holiness;
- to strengthen you for the struggle with evil.'

'You will receive the gift of the Holy Spirit . . . that you may help to bring to the world the fruits of reconciliation and peace. Strengthened by the Holy Spirit and his manifold gifts
- commit yourselves wholeheartedly to the Church's struggle against sin;
- strive to be unselfish;
- try not to be obsessed with material things;
- be active members of the People of God;
- be reconciled with each other;
- be devoted to the work of justice which will bring peace on earth.'

'Young people, the world of today needs you for it needs men and women who are filled with the Holy Spirit. It needs your courage and hopefulness, your faith and your perseverance. The world of tomorrow will be built by you.'

Pentecost Sunday, Coventry, 1982

© Sister Mary Bernard Potter SP and Nigel Bavidge 1993.
Multiple copies of this page may be made by the purchasing church or group only.

COME AND SEE

PRACTICAL DETAILS

Parish of _____

CONFIRMATION PREPARATION 19____

Date of Confirmation _____

Time _____

Place of Confirmation _____

Date of Enrolment Celebration _____

Time _____

Place of Enrolment Celebration _____

Date of Retreat _____

Place of Retreat _____

Date of Election Celebration _____

Time _____

Place of Election Celebration _____

Date of candidates' first meeting _____

Time _____

Place of candidates' first meeting _____

Dates of future meetings (if known)

_____   _____

_____   _____

_____   _____

_____   _____

Confirmation Co-ordinator _____

Telephone no. _____

© Sister Mary Bernard Potter SP and Nigel Bavidge 1993.
Multiple copies of this page may be made by the purchasing church or group only.

Sponsors

You must understand that you are not alone. We are one body, one people, one Church of Christ. The Sponsor who stands at your side represents for you the whole community.

POPE JOHN PAUL II
COVENTRY 1982

© Sister Mary Bernard Potter SP and Nigel Bavidge 1993.
Multiple copies of these pages may be made by the purchasing church or group only.

To be invited to be a sponsor is always a great honour.

It brings with it certain responsibilities, because the sponsor represents the Church, which is calling down God's gifts and blessings on those who are to be confirmed.

Since Confirmation is the completion of Baptism, the Confirmation Sponsor should, ideally, be one of the baptismal godparents.

The Church asks sponsors to become actively involved in the spiritual growth of those whom they are sponsoring by:

- giving an example of Catholic living
- encouraging them to be faithful in their membership of the Church
- praying for them.

This means, therefore, that a sponsor should be a person who is in regular contact and is involved in the life of the person who is to be confirmed. In this way continuing support and encouragement can be given.

You should only accept the invitation to be a sponsor if you are sincerely prepared to accept these responsibilities.

Because the sponsor represents the whole community, to be a sponsor you must be a confirmed and active member of the Catholic Church. Except in unusual circumstances, a sponsor must be not less than 16 years old.

A candidate may choose a sponsor of either sex.

I _____ have been asked to act as Confirmation Sponsor for _____

I am aware of the responsibilities of a sponsor and, with God's help, I am willing to accept them.

Signed _____

Witnessed by _____

Date _____

REQUEST FOR THE ENROLMENT FOR CONFIRMATION

I _____ ask to be enrolled as a candidate for Confirmation.

I promise to do my best to attend all the preparation sessions and the Celebrations.

I ask for the prayers of this, my parish community, to help me to live as a follower of Jesus, and as a witness to the message of the Gospel.

Signed: _____
Witnessed by: _____
Date: _____

© Sister Mary Bernard Potter sp and Nigel Bavidge 1993.
Multiple copies of this page may be made by the purchasing church or group only.

Parent Promise

I promise to continue to support and encourage my child _____
in preparing for the Sacrament of Confirmation.

I ask for the prayers of my parish community, to help me to continue to give good example, clear guidance and loving care to my child.

Signed: _____
Witnessed by: _____
Date: _____

© Sister Mary Bernard Potter SP and Nigel Bavidge 1993.
Multiple copies of this page may be made by the purchasing church or group only.

Unit 1

Getting to Know You

Unit aims

1. To begin to develop a sense of community.
2. To introduce candidates to each other and to the catechists.
3. To gather the information necessary for subsequent meetings.

Outline

1. Welcome and prayer (*2 mins*)
2. Introductions (*5 mins*)
3. 'Fish and Chips' game (pairs) (*5 mins*)
4. 'Who are You?' handout (*20 mins*)
5. Problem-solving exercises (*20 mins*)
6. Refreshment break (*15 mins*)
7. Catechists and their groups (*15 mins*)
8. Prayer (*5 mins*)
9. Conclusion (*3 mins*)

Materials

'Prayer sheet' (*handout on p. 35*)

'Fish and Chips' cards (*handouts on pp. 36–37*)

'Who are You?' (*handout on p. 38 or p. 39*)

'The Maze' (*handout on p. 40*)

or

'Your Orders' (*handout on p. 41*)

and

'Map' (*handout on p. 42*)

'Letter' (*handout on p. 43*)

or

'Letter' (*handout on p. 44*)

Pens and pencils

Long strips of paper about 2 inches wide and blindfolds for 'The Maze' (if used)

Tape recorder and tape

Hymn books

page 31

Welcome the Spirit

PREPARATION

- Prepare the focal point, e.g. table with red/white cloth on which is placed the open Bible, an attractive and reasonably sized candle and a plant or flower arrangement. If a display screen is available, surround the text 'We are one in the Spirit' with pictures of a wide variety of people
- Prepare the room—chairs in one large circle or semicircle
- Refreshments.

SESSION

1. Welcome and prayer

- The chief catechist should welcome everyone and introduce herself/himself to the group.
- Distribute the handout on p. 35, 'Prayer sheet'.
- Lead into the prayer using an introduction along these lines:

    God, you are father and mother to us all, we turn to you in prayer as we say ... pour out ...

(Remember that there are many titles of God, which point to different aspects of the mystery of God, e.g. Creator, Life-giver, Father, Mother, All-powerful, God of love, of life, of mercy, of power, etc. By using different ways of addressing God you can help people to be more aware of the infinite nature of God.)

- Say the prayer together:

    ... pour out your Spirit
    upon your people,
    and grant us
    a new vision of your glory,
    a new experience of your power,
    a new faithfulness to your Word,
    a new consecration to your service,
    that your love may grow among us,
    and your kingdom come;
    through Christ, our Lord.
    Amen.

2. Introductions

- The other catechists should introduce themselves.

3. 'Fish and Chips' game

- Distribute handouts on pp. 36–37, 'Fish and Chips' cards.

Unit One: *Getting to Know You*

- Invite each person to find their matching partner, e.g. 'fish' finds 'chips'.

  (*Have one of the catechists ready to take part in this activity if there is an uneven number participating.*)

4. 'Who are You?'

- Distribute *either* the handout on p. 38, 'Who are You?' (for candidates aged 13/14 years) *or* the handout on p. 39, 'Who are You?' (for candidates aged 15/16 years). Ask each pair to complete the questionnaire by interviewing each other. Allow about 10 minutes for this activity.

- Ask each pair to meet another pair and, using the information from the handout, each person introduces his/her partner.

5. Problem-solving exercises

- The aim of these exercises is to give the candidates an opportunity to work together and help to build up a sense of community.

either

- **An exercise for pairs**
  Distribute to each pair the handout on p. 40, 'The Maze', with long strips of paper and a blindfold.

or

- **An exercise for groups of three or four**
  Distribute to each group the handout on p. 41, 'Your Orders', and the handout on p. 42, 'The Map'. (This second exercise may be more suitable for older candidates.)

6. Refreshment break

7. Catechists and their groups

- Each catechist now meets his/her own group of candidates to get to know them and to arrange future meetings.

- If the groups are going to meet in the catechists' homes, then dates and times of meetings will have to be negotiated. The handout on p. 43, 'The Letter', should be distributed, asking the candidates the name of the parent or guardian to whom the letter should be addressed.

- If the groups are going to meet in the parish hall use the handout on p. 44, 'The Letter'.

When arrangements are made for the sessions to take place in the catechists' homes it is vital that the catechists should work in pairs.

8. Prayer

- Invite the group to gather round the prayer table.
- Begin by playing a piece of quiet music, e.g. Taizé *'Veni Sancte Spiritus'*.

- Say the following invitation to prayer or compose one:

    Let us be still and know that God is with us ... (music continues ... and then fades out before the reading).

- Reading (1 Corinthians 12:12):

    **Christ is like a single body,
    which has many parts;
    it is still one body,
    even though it is made up of different parts.
    All of you are Christ's body,
    and each one is a part of it.**

- Short pause for silent reflection.
- The catechist shares a few words on the meaning of the reading.
- Sign of peace

    As a sign of our belonging together let us offer each other a sign of our friendship.

- Hymn, e.g. 'Bind Us Together'.

9. Conclusion

- Thank the candidates for coming to the session.
- Remind them to deliver the letter about the future sessions.
- Remind the candidates about the 'Request for Enrolment' and 'Parent Promise', which were distributed at the introductory session.

Team reflection

1. Did the session go well? Make a note of any adaptations you would recommend for future use.
2. Have any problems emerged? How can they be dealt with?

Session Prayer

This is the prayer which will be used at the beginning of each session. We turn to God, who loves us, and ask for the gift of the Holy Spirit:

. . . pour out your Spirit
upon your people,
and grant us
a new vision of your glory,
a new experience of your power,
a new faithfulness to your word,
a new consecration to your service,
that your love may grow among us,
and your kingdom come;
through Christ, our Lord.
Amen.

© Sister Mary Bernard Potter SP and Nigel Bavidge 1993.
Multiple copies of this page may be made by the purchasing church or group only.

Cut out triangular shapes.

FOOD

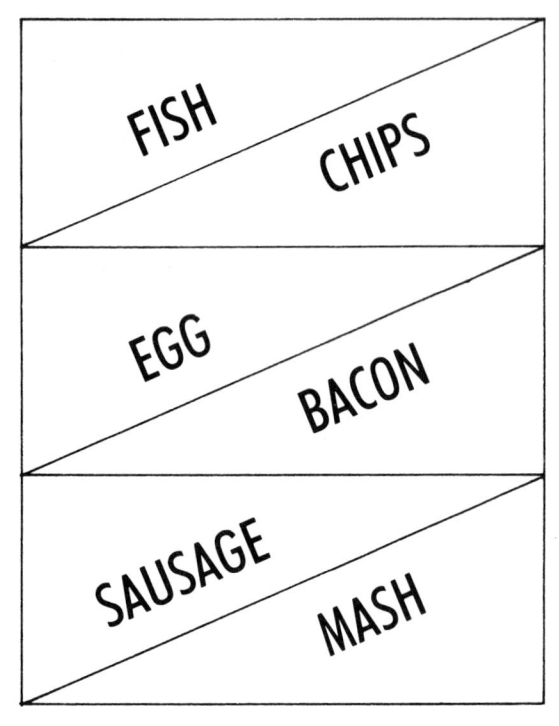

- FISH / CHIPS
- EGG / BACON
- SAUSAGE / MASH

SPORTS GEAR

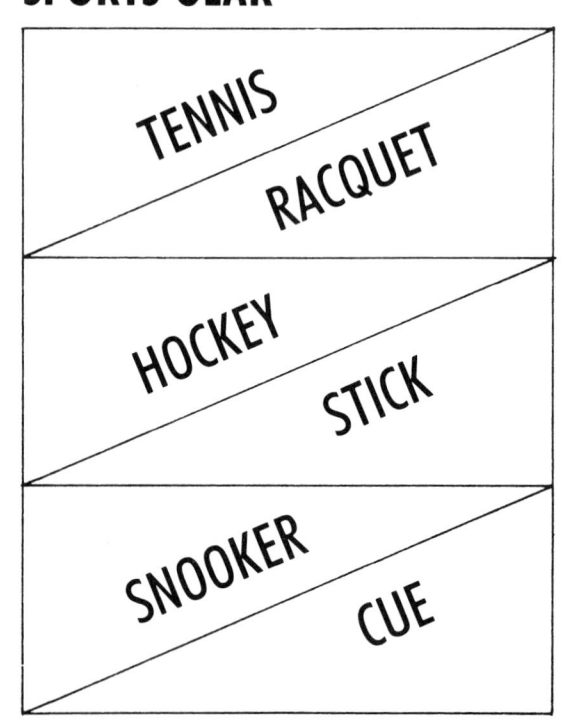

- TENNIS / RACQUET
- HOCKEY / STICK
- SNOOKER / CUE

FOOTBALL CLUBS

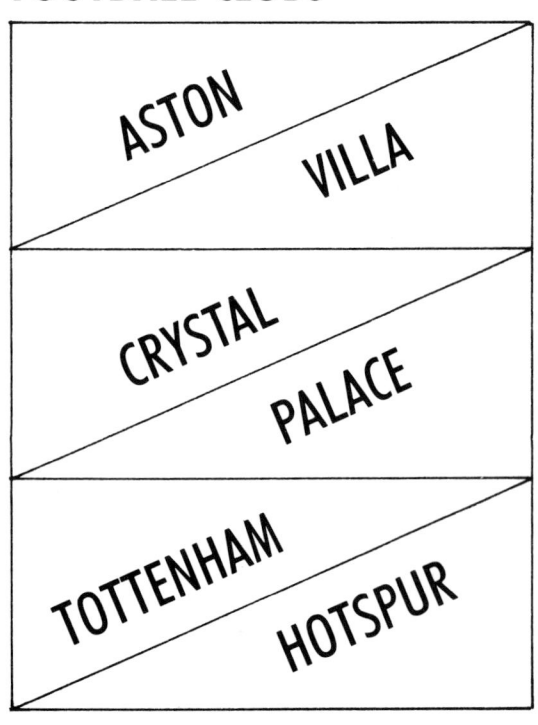

- ASTON / VILLA
- CRYSTAL / PALACE
- TOTTENHAM / HOTSPUR

TV PROGRAMMES

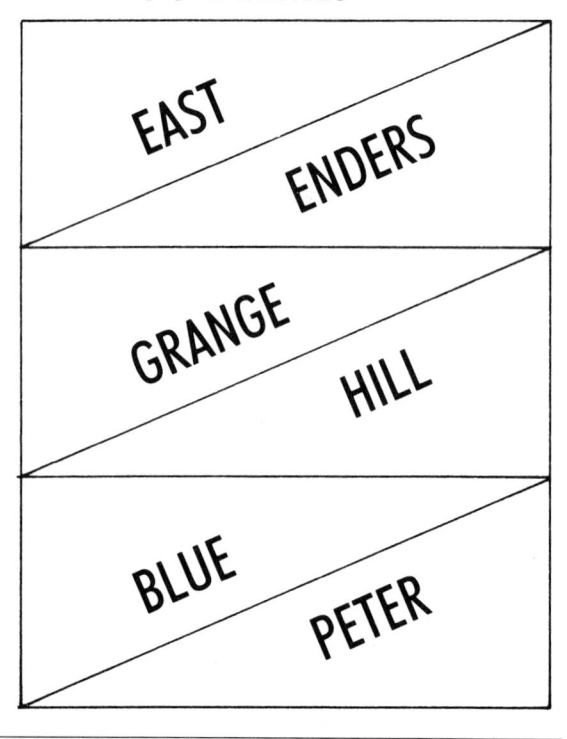

- EAST / ENDERS
- GRANGE / HILL
- BLUE / PETER

© Sister Mary Bernard Potter SP and Nigel Bavidge 1993.
Multiple copies of this page may be made by the purchasing church or group only.

Cut out triangular shapes.

RIVERS

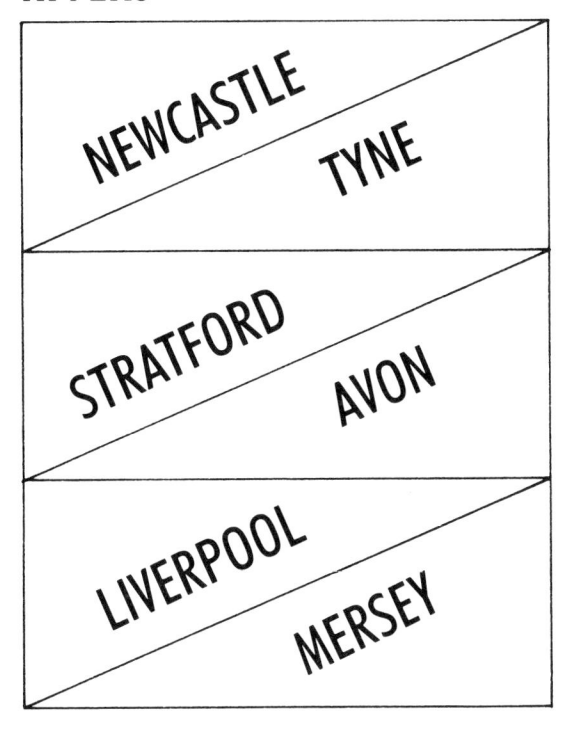

- NEWCASTLE / TYNE
- STRATFORD / AVON
- LIVERPOOL / MERSEY

COMEDIANS

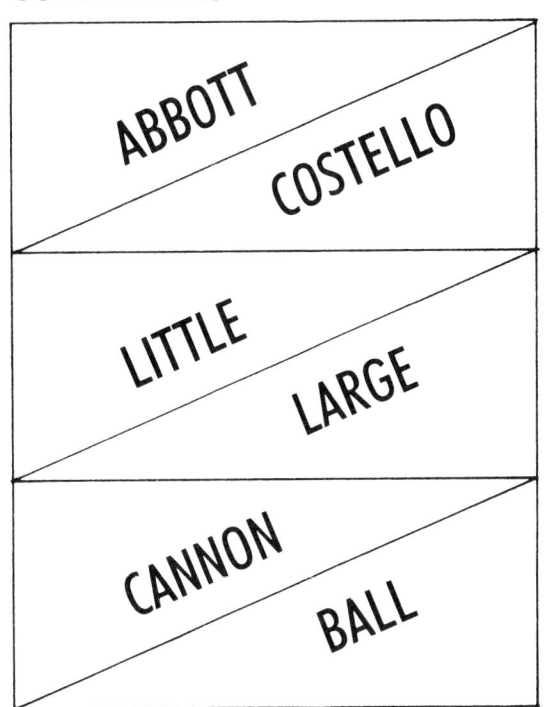

- ABBOTT / COSTELLO
- LITTLE / LARGE
- CANNON / BALL

CAPITAL CITIES

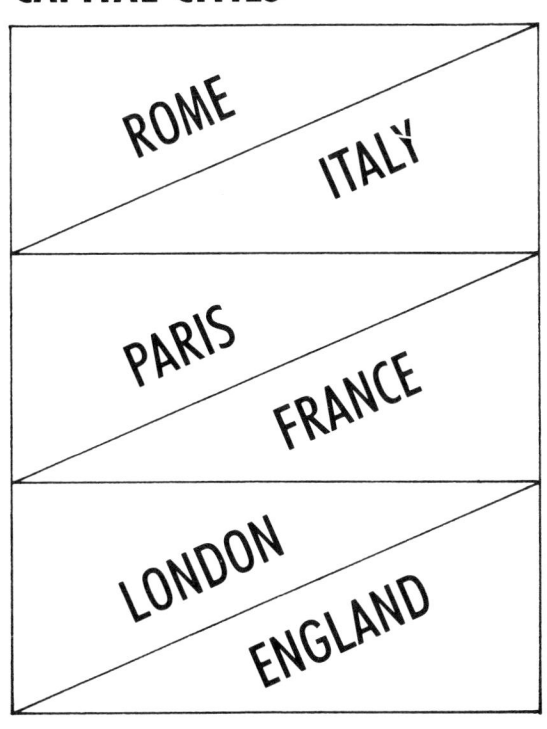

- ROME / ITALY
- PARIS / FRANCE
- LONDON / ENGLAND

ANIMALS

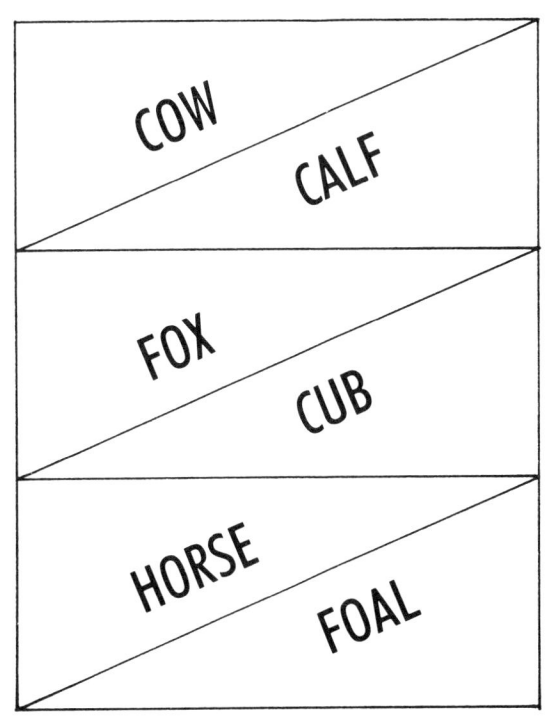

- COW / CALF
- FOX / CUB
- HORSE / FOAL

© Sister Mary Bernard Potter sp and Nigel Bavidge 1993.
Multiple copies of this page may be made by the purchasing church or group only.

GETTING TO KNOW YOU

WHO ARE YOU?

Find out about your partner

What is your name? _____

How old are you? _____

When is your birthday? _____

Who are the members of your family? _____

Do you have any pets? _____

What do you do in your free time? _____

What kind of music do you dislike most? _____

What is your favourite group? _____

Are you interested in sports? _____

Do you support any teams? _____

What school do you go to? _____

What subject are you best at? _____

What is your worst subject? _____

What is your favourite food? _____

What kind of clothes do you like to wear? _____

What is your favourite TV programme? _____

Have you a favourite magazine? _____

If you had £50, how would you spend it? _____

How would you describe the kind of person you are?

- ☐ easy going?
- ☐ noisy and bouncy?
- ☐ hard working?
- ☐ sports loving?
- ☐ tidy and organized?

- ☐ quiet and shy?
- ☐ fairly serious?
- ☐ good at making friends?
- ☐ trendy?
- ☐ messy?

Are there any other things you would like to add to this list about yourself?

© Sister Mary Bernard Potter SP and Nigel Bavidge 1993.
Multiple copies of this page may be made by the purchasing church or group only.

GETTING TO KNOW YOU

Who are you?

Find out about your partner

What is your name? _____

What do you like most and dislike most about school? _____
_____

What do you hope to do after GCSE? _____
_____

What do you do in your free time? _____
_____

What, for you, makes a good evening out? _____
_____

What things make you angry? _____
_____

What concerns you most about the future of our society? _____
_____

How would you describe the kind of person you are?

☐ easy going? ☐ quiet and shy?
☐ hardworking? ☐ fairly serious?
☐ sports loving? ☐ good at making friends?
☐ tidy and organized? ☐ laid back?

Are there any other things you would like to add to this list about yourself?

_____
_____
_____

© Sister Mary Bernard Potter sp and Nigel Bavidge 1993.
Multiple copies of this page may be made by the purchasing church or group only.

GETTING TO KNOW YOU

THE MAZE

1. One of you lays out a maze, using long strips of paper to make the path to the treasure at the end of the maze.

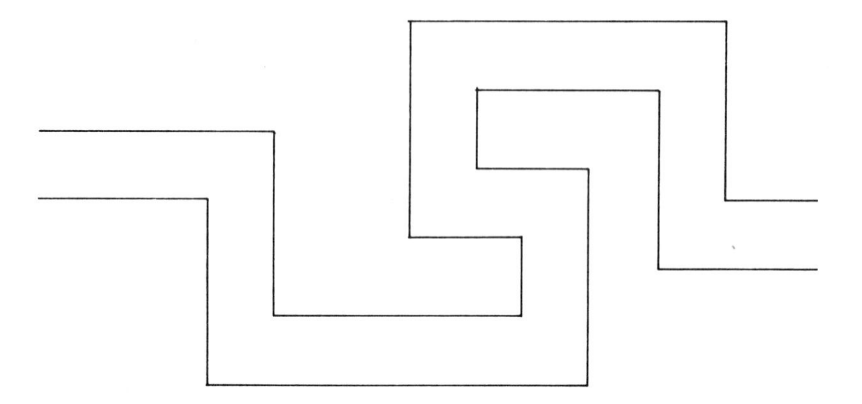

2. The other of you has to go through the maze, blindfolded, but should you walk on or over the maze lines you will be disintegrated!

3. The one who laid out the maze can give you instructions to get you through the maze, but he/she *cannot* use words or touch you or lead you.

4. You have 3 minutes to work out how you are going to get through the maze.

© Sister Mary Bernard Potter sp and Nigel Bavidge 1993.
Multiple copies of this page may be made by the purchasing church or group only.

GETTING TO KNOW YOU

Your orders

- Leaving base camp at 6 a.m. on Day 1 you must go to the island to collect the stolen code.

- You must be at the *rendezvous* point with the code by 12 noon on Day 3.

- The estimated distances are on your map.

- Sunset on Day 1 will be at 9.30 p.m.
  Sunset on Day 2 will be at 9.15 p.m.

- Sunrise on Day 2 will be at 5.45 a.m.
  Sunrise on Day 3 will be at 5.50 a.m.

- Mid-day temperature averages 38 degrees Centigrade.

- Night temperature is 5 degrees Centigrade.

- You have a choice of equipment but you are only permitted to take six items with you.

What will you take?

You must select only six items from this list.

☐	First aid kit	☐	Climbing rope and pegs
☐	Wellingtons	☐	Inflatable dinghy
☐	Walking boots	☐	Compass
☐	Water bottle	☐	Foil survival capes
☐	Sleeping bags	☐	Distress flare
☐	Thermos flask	☐	Water purifying tablets
☐	Insect repellent	☐	Gun and ammunition
☐	Dehydrated food	☐	Money
☐	Map	☐	Sun glasses
☐	Firelighters	☐	Torch
☐	Chocolate	☐	Matches

Will you survive?

© Sister Mary Bernard Potter sp and Nigel Bavidge 1993.
Multiple copies of this page may be made by the purchasing church or group only.

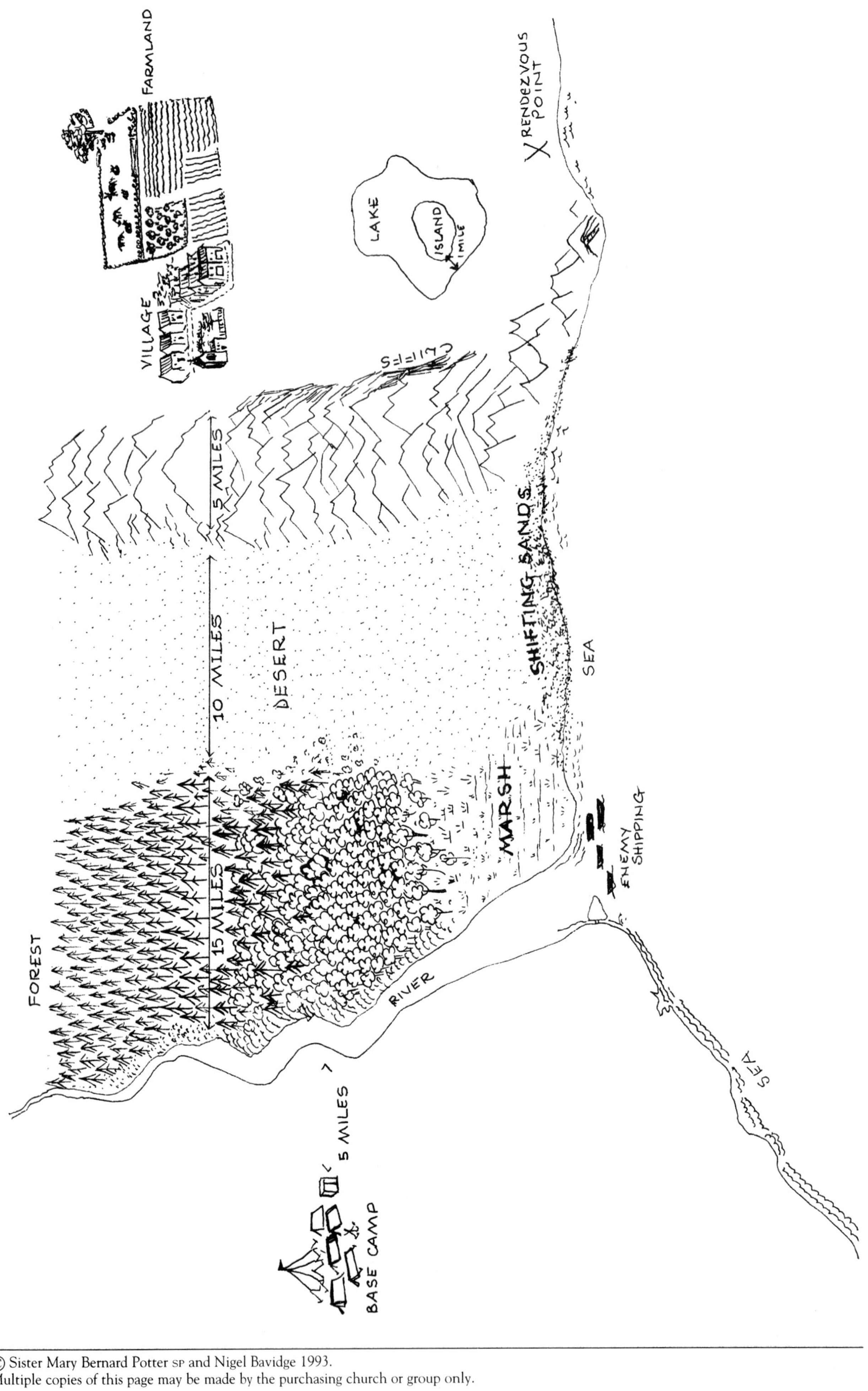
FARMLAND
VILLAGE
LAKE
ISLAND
1 MILE
RENDEZVOUS POINT
CLIFFS
5 MILES
10 MILES
15 MILES
DESERT
SHIFTING SANDS
SEA
MARSH
ENEMY SHIPPING
FOREST
RIVER
SEA
5 MILES
BASE CAMP

(Church address)

Dear

Now that we have had our first meeting with the Confirmation Candidates, we have been able to arrange the place, times and dates of future meetings.

Your son's/daughter's catechist is:

_____

The meetings will take place at the home of:

Name _____

Address _____

_____

Telephone no. _____

The meetings will be on:

Day   **Date**   **Time** (from–to)

We hope you are happy with these arrangements. If there are any queries please do not hesitate to contact the catechist.

Yours sincerely,

Confirmation Co-ordinator

© Sister Mary Bernard Potter sp and Nigel Bavidge 1993.
Multiple copies of this page may be made by the purchasing church or group only.

(Church address)

Dear

Now that we have had our first meeting with the Confirmation Candidates, we have been able to arrange the place, times and dates of future meetings.

Your son's/daughter's catechist is:

_____

Telephone no. _____

The meetings will take place in the Parish Hall.
The meetings will be on:

Day   **Date**   **Time** (from–to)

We hope you are happy with these arrangements. If there are any queries please do not hesitate to contact the catechist.

Yours sincerely,

Confirmation Co-ordinator

© Sister Mary Bernard Potter SP and Nigel Bavidge 1993.
Multiple copies of this page may be made by the purchasing church or group only.

Unit 2

BELONGING

UNIT AIMS

1. To explore the experience of belonging.
2. To explore the human need to belong.
3. To examine the responsibilities which come with belonging.
4. To link the human experience of belonging to the sacramental life of the Church.
5. To examine the responsibilities of belonging to the Church.

OUTLINE

1. Welcome and prayer (*3 mins*)
2. Introductions (*3 mins*)
3. Presentation and activities I (*35 mins*)
4. Refreshment break (*10 mins*)
5. Presentation and activities II (*20 mins*)
6. Prayer (*10 mins*)
7. Conclusion (*10 mins*)

MATERIALS

'I Belong' (*handout on p. 50*)
'Think and Share' (*handout on p. 51*)
'Responsibilities' (*handout on p. 52*)
'Who is Jesus?' (*handout on p. 53*)
Prayer of St Richard ('Day by Day') (*handout on p. 54*)
'A Letter' (*handout on p. 55*)
'I Have Called You by Name' (*handout on pp. 56–57*)

Large sheets of paper
Felt-tip pens, pencils and pens
If it is not possible to prepare the display recommended in Unit Preparation it is essential to make a poster using the same words 'People who need people are the luckiest people in the world' and to surround the caption with pictures of groups of people.
Tape recorder and music
Copies of the Bible – one for each candidate

page 45

Welcome the Spirit

PREPARATION

- Prepare a focal point, e.g. table with red/white cloth on which is placed the open Bible, an attractive and reasonably sized candle and a plant or flower arrangement. If a display screen is available, surround the caption 'People who need people are the luckiest people in the world' with pictures of groups of people.
- Set tape recorder correctly.
- Refreshments.

SESSION

1. Welcome and prayer

- The catechists welcome everyone.
- Using the handout on p. 35, introduce and say the prayer together. This handout should be in the candidates' files, though it may be advisable to have a few spare copies available!

> … pour out your Spirit
> upon your people,
> and grant us
> a new vision of your glory,
> a new experience of your power,
> a new faithfulness to your Word,
> a new consecration to your service,
> that your love may grow among us,
> and your kingdom come;
> through Christ, our Lord.
> Amen.

2. Introductions

- Ensure the candidates and catechists all know each other.

[Handwritten note: Consider general aspects of belonging to a group. Church in particular. Confirmation's relationship to the group/community that is the Church.]

3. Presentation and activities 1

Short presentation by catechist:

- Refer to the display 'People who need people'. Ask the group what they think this means and whether they agree with the idea.
- Linking their responses, the catechist should say something like this:

> We all need people. Without others we could not survive. I think of all the different people who have helped me to become me. (Name some examples.) Some of the people I mentioned belonged to my family, others to the place where I work/live. Others are members of my parish, others belong to clubs/

organizations I belong to. All of us belong to various groups. All of us here belong to a family and a church. All of you belong to a school. You have friends. Some of you belong to clubs or teams.

- Ask the candidates to identify the groups to which they belong using the handout on p. 50, 'I Belong'. Allow time for the candidates to complete their lists and then invite them to share their lists with one other person.

- On large sheets of paper, on which are written the three headings which are on the handout on p. 50, list the groups which the candidates have named.

- Distribute the handout on p. 51, 'Think and Share'. Ask the candidates to complete the task and to share their thoughts with one other person.

- Take some examples from the candidates' findings and, on large sheets of paper, list with them:
  — the *benefits* of belonging to groups
  — the *responsibilities* of belonging to groups.

4. Refreshment break

5. Presentation and activities II

- Linking the ideas from Presentation and activities I, the catechist should say something like this:

    We have seen that we all belong to groups of one kind or another. Some of the groups we belong to by *choice*, others we had *no choice* about. But, even though we had no choice, these groups still matter to us—we certainly couldn't manage without our families for example.

    One of the groups we belong to is the Church. When your parents asked to have you baptized they made a choice. They wanted you to come to know Jesus Christ by belonging to the Church as a child of God. You will always belong to God's family.

    Asking to have a baby baptized is a very serious responsibility. Let's look at some parts of the Baptism ceremony to see what your parents chose for you and what responsibilities they took on.

- Distribute the handout on p. 52, 'Responsibilities', ask the candidates, working in pairs, to identify the benefits and responsibilities accepted at Baptism.
    When this has been done, gather all the ideas and list them on a large sheet of paper. Summarize for the group the ideas given up to this point:
    — we all need people
    — we all belong to groups
    — groups give us lots of benefits
    — we have responsibilities when we belong to a group
    — as a member of God's family, the Church, we have support, help, guidance, etc. (use words from the list)
    — we will now look more closely at what our Baptism should mean for us.

- Another word for Baptism is 'Christening'. What do you think that means? (Allow candidates time to answer.) It means that God calls us to become like Jesus Christ. Jesus Christ is the person we try to model our lives on, we try to become like him
    — in all we do
    — in all we say

Welcome the Spirit

— in the way we think
— in the way we act.

To be able to model our lives on Jesus, we must know him. How can we come to know him? List the candidates' responses, which should include:

— Prayer
— Scripture
— Other people
— The Church.

One of our most important ways of coming to know Jesus is to look at the stories about him in the Gospels. Distribute the handout on p. 53, 'Who is Jesus?' and copies of the Bible. Ask the candidates, working in pairs, to complete the handout.

Draw together the candidates' ideas.

6. Prayer

- Distribute the handout on p. 54, 'Prayer of St Richard'.

- Begin by playing quiet music.

- Over the music say:

    Lord Jesus Christ,
    you have come among us
    to show us how to live.
    Help us to live and love like you,
      in our homes,
      in our schools,
      with our friends,
      and with all those we know.
      Amen.

- Reading from John's Gospel:

    Jesus said:
    'You did not choose me, I chose you.
    If you love me you will keep my
    commandments.
    I will ask the Father and he will give you
    another Helper who will stay with you for
    ever.
    Whoever accepts my commandments
    and obeys them
    is the one who loves me.'

- Short pause for silent reflection.

- Say together:

    Day by day,
    three things I pray,
    to see you more clearly,
    love you more dearly,
    and follow you more nearly.

- Hymn, e.g. 'Let There Be Love'.
    (We suggest that you substitute the word 'family' for 'brotherly' throughout the hymn!)

page 48

7. Conclusion

- Remind candidates about the Enrolment Celebration. Explain that this is their choice. God has chosen them to belong to the family of the Church, but they must also choose God. It might be helpful to read through the ceremony with them.

- Remind them to bring 'Request for Enrolment' and ask them to remind their parents to bring 'Parent Promise' to the Enrolment Celebration.

- Distribute the handout on p. 55, 'A Letter' and ask the candidates to complete it at home and bring it with them in their file to the next meeting.

- Similarly, distribute the handout on pp. 56–57, 'I Have Called You by Name', and ask the candidates to complete it over the next few weeks. It will be referred to next in Unit Six, 'You Will Be My Witnesses'.

Team reflection

1. Did the session go well? Make a note of any adaptations you would recommend for future use.
2. Have any problems emerged? How can they be dealt with?

BELONGING

I BELONG

Everyone belongs to lots of different groups:

> FAMILY
>
> NATION
>
> WORLD

We are born into these groups.

There are other groups to which we belong. Some we choose to belong to. Others, the choice was made for us. List the groups you belong to.

A Groups I belong to because I was born into them	B Groups I belong to because someone made the choice for me	C Groups I belong to because I made my own choice

© Sister Mary Bernard Potter SP and Nigel Bavidge 1993.
Multiple copies of this page may be made by the purchasing church or group only.

BELONGING

THINK AND SHARE

Choose one group from Section B on your Handout 'I Belong'.

Name of Group _____

What are the benefits of belonging to this group?

What do you have to do for the group? What are the responsibilities that go with belonging to this group?

What had to happen for you to belong to the group?

Now choose a group from Section C.

Name of Group _____

What are the benefits of belonging to this group?

What do you have to do for the group? What are the responsibilities that go with belonging to this group?

What had to happen for you to belong to the group?

© Sister Mary Bernard Potter sp and Nigel Bavidge 1993.
Multiple copies of this page may be made by the purchasing church or group only.

BELONGING

RESPONSIBILITIES

What is the priest saying about belonging?

_____
_____
_____

> The Christian community welcomes you with great joy and in its name I claim you for Christ our Saviour

> You have asked to have your child baptized. In doing so you are accepting the responsibility of bringing her/him up in the practice of the faith. It will be your duty to bring her/him up to keep God's commandments as Christ taught us, by loving God and our neighbour

What did your family agree to do?

_____
_____
_____

What responsibility did your family take on when you were baptized?

_____
_____

Now you are no longer a baby what do you have to do?

_____
_____
_____

What **choices** and what **responsibilities** are now yours?

_____
_____
_____

> This light is entrusted to you to be kept burning brightly

© Sister Mary Bernard Potter SP and Nigel Bavidge 1993.
Multiple copies of this page may be made by the purchasing church or group only.

BELONGING

WHO IS JESUS?

We don't really know what Jesus looks like

but

we do know the kind of person Jesus was. We know this from the Gospels. Try to complete these circles which illustrate some of the qualities of Jesus. One has been done for you.

QUALITY: Leadership
STORY: The call of the disciples
THE STORY IS IN: St Mark's Gospel, chapter 1, verses 16-20

QUALITY: _____
STORY: _____
THE STORY IS IN: St John's Gospel, chapter 13, verses 1-15

QUALITY: _____
STORY: _____
THE STORY IS IN: St Mark's Gospel, chapter 10, verses 46-52

QUALITY: _____
STORY: _____
THE STORY IS IN: St Luke's Gospel, chapter 7, verses 11-17

QUALITY: _____
STORY: _____
THE STORY IS IN: St Luke's Gospel, chapter 22, verses 33-34

© Sister Mary Bernard Potter SP and Nigel Bavidge 1993.
Multiple copies of this page may be made by the purchasing church or group only.

PRAYER OF ST RICHARD

Day by day,
three things I pray,
to see you more clearly,
love you more dearly,
and to follow you more nearly.

A LETTER

You have a letter from a friend. In it your friend says:

> I know that you are a Catholic and believe in Jesus.
> I don't know much about him.
> I know that he lived and died about 2,000 years ago but I really don't know what kind of person Jesus was. What do you think about him? How do you see him?

What would you say in your reply?

BELONGING

'I HAVE CALLED YOU BY NAME'

What is your full name? _____

Ask why these names were chosen for you.

What were the reasons?

_____
_____
_____

Our names are very important to us because they identify us as special and unique.

We are special and unique to God, who knows each of us by name. In the Bible we read:

> I have called you by name.
> You are precious in my eyes.
> You are mine
> and I love you.
>
> *(cf. Isaiah 43:1)*

When we are confirmed the Bishop says our name and then adds: 'Be sealed with the gift of the Holy Spirit.'

The name by which the Bishop calls us can be the name given to us by our parents, provided that it is the name of one of the saints or of the holy women or men in the Bible.

Alternatively you can choose a new name taking the name of one of the saints or of a holy person in the Bible.

What do you think?

_____
_____
_____

© Sister Mary Bernard Potter SP and Nigel Bavidge 1993.
Multiple copies of this page may be made by the purchasing church or group only.

'I HAVE CALLED YOU BY NAME' (CONTINUED)

Our Confirmation name (even if it is the same as our baptismal name) reminds us:
- — we are special to God
- — we are part of the family of the Church which includes not only the people of today, but also all those who are now with God in heaven (Communion of Saints).

When we choose our Confirmation name we are linked in a special way with that holy person and we can be sure that they will pray for us.

What name are you going to choose? _____

Why have you chosen this name? _____
_____

What can you find out about the life of this person?
_____
_____
_____
_____

Does your saint have a special day (Feast Day)?
_____

You might find information in your school library, or the public library may have a dictionary of saints (e.g. *The Penguin Dictionary of Saints*).

© Sister Mary Bernard Potter SP and Nigel Bavidge 1993.
Multiple copies of this page may be made by the purchasing church or group only.

Celebration of Enrolment

Celebration Aims

This celebration is an important part of the preparation of the Confirmation candidates.

Its purposes are:

1. To emphasize the importance of the step which the candidates are taking.

2. To highlight that the candidates are making the decision to be confirmed of their own free choice.

3. To bring to the attention of the whole parish community the responsibilities they have towards the candidates.

Outline

This celebration should take place during one particular Sunday Eucharist in the parish or at the Sunday Eucharist which the candidates normally attend.

The Enrolment is celebrated after the Creed.

A sample text for an Enrolment Celebration is given in this section and on the handout on pp. 62–65. It is suggested that the name of the parish and the date of the Celebration of Enrolment should be added to the front of the cover, and the names of the candidates to the back of the cover, before photocopying.

Photocopy pp. 62–65 onto A4 paper, turn sideways and assemble into a booklet. Pages (2) and (7) should be photocopied onto the back of pages (1) and (8), and pages (6) and (3) onto the backs of pages (4) and (5). Check that the back and front of each page will come out the same way up.

STRUCTURE

- Introduction
- Prayer
- Presentation of the Candidates
- Enquiry: Candidates
  Families
  Parish Community
- Acceptance

It would be a good idea to follow up this liturgical celebration with some social event.

MATERIALS

- The candidates should bring the handout on p. 29, 'Request for Enrolment' and their families should bring the handout on p. 30, 'Parent Promise'.
- It would be advisable to have spare copies of these documents available in case of necessity.
- Copies of the Celebration of Enrolment for everyone.

The Celebration of Enrolment of Candidates for the Sacrament of Confirmation

Introduction

Priest: My brothers and sisters, today we celebrate the fact that God is calling members of our parish community to deepen their faith and their commitment. These young people were brought into new life through Baptism and now they are being called by God to open their hearts to receive the gift of the Holy Spirit. The sacraments are God's great gift to us. They are the ways in which we become more and more like Jesus and they call us to a life of prayer and service. To ask to receive a sacrament is, therefore, a solemn and serious step to take.

Today these young people are taking this step and we welcome them and must support them with our prayers and example.

Prayer

Priest: Let us pray then.

God of love
pour out your blessing on these young people,
fill them with the power of your love
so that they may open their minds and hearts
to hear your call
and respond with generosity
to the gifts you offer.
We make our prayer through Christ, our Lord.

Congregation: Amen.

Presentation of the candidates

Catechist: Father, I present to you these young people who ask to be prepared for the Sacrament of Confirmation.

I present to you and to this whole community N . . .

(As each name is called the candidate goes to the priest and presents the 'Request for Enrolment' document.)

Enquiry

Addressing the candidates the priest asks:

Priest: Do you wish to be enrolled as a candidate for the sacrament of Confirmation?

Candidates: I do.

Celebration of Enrolment

Priest: Do you promise to take part in our parish preparation for the sacrament?

Candidates: I do.

Priest: What do you ask of this parish?

Candidates: I ask for the prayers and support of the parish.

Addressing the candidates' families:

Priest: I now invite the families of the candidates to stand.

In the name of God and this parish I thank you for the support and love which you have shown to these young people. Your encouragement and example have brought them to this day. I now ask you:

Do you promise to continue this good work and give these young people all the support and help which they will need to have as followers of our Lord, Jesus Christ?

Families: We do.

Priest: I now invite a member of the family to present to me their 'Parent Promise' document.

Addressing the parish community, the priest asks:

Priest: I now ask you all, the whole congregation, having heard the requests and the promises made by these members of our community, are you willing and ready to support and guide these candidates for the Sacrament of Confirmation by your prayers, example and personal witness of faith?

Congregation: We are.

Acceptance

Addressing the candidates once more, the priest says:

Priest: My dear young people,
The whole community welcomes you with joy.
You are now solemnly enrolled as candidates for Confirmation.
May God, who has begun this great work in you
bring you to an ever deeper love
and openness to the gifts
which are offered to you.
We make this prayer through Christ, our Lord.

Congregation: Amen.

Celebration of Enrolment of Candidates for Confirmation

Parish of _____

Date _____

CANDIDATES' NAMES

© Sister Mary Bernard Potter sp and Nigel Bavidge 1993.
Multiple copies of these pages may be made by the purchasing church or group only.

This Celebration of Enrolment is an important part of the parish preparation of the candidates for the Sacrament of Confirmation.

The purposes of the Celebration are:

- to emphasize the importance of the step which the candidates are taking

- to highlight that the candidates are making the decision to be confirmed of their own free choice

- to bring to the attention of the whole parish community the responsibilities they have towards the candidates.

CELEBRATION OF ENROLMENT

Introduction

Priest: My brothers and sisters, today we celebrate the fact that God is calling members of our parish community to deepen their faith and their commitment. These young people were brought into new life through Baptism and now they are being called by God to open their hearts to receive the gift of the Holy Spirit. The sacraments are God's great gift to us. They are the ways in which we become more and more like Jesus and they call us to a life of prayer and service. To ask to receive a sacrament is, therefore, a solemn and serious step to take.

Today these young people are taking this step and we welcome them and must support them with our prayers and example.

Prayer

Priest: Let us pray then.
God of love
pour out your blessing on these young people,
fill them with the power of your love
so that they may open their minds and hearts
to hear your call
and respond with generosity
to the gifts you offer.
We make our prayer through Christ, our Lord.

Congregation: Amen.

Presentation of the candidates

Catechist: Father, I present to you these young people who ask to be prepared for the Sacrament of Confirmation.

I present to you and to this whole community N . . .

(As each name is called the candidate goes to the priest and presents the 'Request for Enrolment' document.)

Enquiry

Addressing the candidates the priest asks:

Priest: Do you wish to be enrolled as a candidate for the Sacrament of Confirmation?

Candidates: I do.

Priest: Do you promise to take part in our parish preparation for the sacrament?

Candidates: I do.

Priest: What do you ask of this parish?

Candidates: I ask for the prayers and support of the parish.

Addressing the candidates' families:

Priest: I now invite the families of the candidates to stand.

In the name of God and this parish I thank you for the support and love which you have shown to these young people. Your encouragement and example have brought them to this day. I now ask you:

Do you promise to continue this good work and give these young people all the support and help which they will need to have as followers of our Lord, Jesus Christ?

Families: We do.

Priest: I now invite a member of the family to present to me their 'Parent Promise' document.

Addressing the parish community, the priest asks:

Priest: I now ask you all, the whole congregation, having heard the requests and the promises made by these members of our community, are you willing and ready to support and guide these candidates for the Sacrament of Confirmation by your prayers, example and personal witness of faith?

Congregation: We are.

Acceptance

Addressing the candidates once more, the priest says:

Priest: My dear young people,
the whole community welcomes you with joy.
You are now solemnly enrolled as candidates for Confirmation.
May God, who has begun this great work in you bring you to an ever deeper love and openness to the gifts which are offered to you.
We make this prayer through Christ, our Lord.

Congregation: Amen.

Unit 3

Sign and Symbol

Unit Aims

1. To examine the meaning of sign and the meaning of symbol.
2. To heighten awareness of God's self-communication through signs and symbols.
3. To explore the concept of Sacrament as an effective sign of God's activity.

Outline

1. Welcome and prayer (*3 mins*)
2. Reflection on the Celebration of Enrolment (*10 mins*)
3. Presentation and activities I (*35 mins*)
4. Refreshment break (*10 mins*)
5. Presentation and activities II (*20 mins*)
6. Prayer (*5 mins*)
7. Conclusion (*5 mins*)

Materials

'Signs' (*handout on p. 71*)
'Body Language' (*handout on p. 72*)
'Gospel Search' (*handout on p. 73*)
'Sign or Symbol?' (*handout on p. 74*)
'Link the Sacrament, the Picture and the Action' (*handout on p. 75*)

'An Interview' (*handout on p. 76*)
Large sheets of paper
Felt-tip pens, pencils and pens
Tape recorder and music tape
Hymn books

Unit Three: Sign and Symbol

PREPARATION

- Tape recorder set correctly.
- Refreshments.
- Prepare a focal point—Title 'God shows us love'—surround the caption with pictures of: nature, people, ikon of Christ, sacramental celebrations.

SESSION

1. Welcome and prayer

- The catechists welcome everyone.
- Using the handout on p. 35, introduce and say the prayer together. This handout should be in the candidates' files, though it may be advisable to have a few spare copies available!

> ... pour out your Spirit
> upon your people,
> and grant us
> a new vision of your glory,
> a new experience of your power,
> a new faithfulness to your Word,
> a new consecration to your service,
> that your love may grow among us,
> and your kingdom come;
> through Christ, our Lord.
> Amen.

2. Reflection on the Celebration of Enrolment

- The catechist reflects with the candidates on the Celebration of Enrolment, inviting them to share their thoughts and feelings about the celebration, for example:

  Did you enjoy the Celebration?
  Was this an important thing to do?
  Why was it important?

- The catechist should then say:

  The Enrolment Celebration was a *symbol* that you want to be part of the Confirmation Preparation Programme. By giving your name and signing the document you showed that this is what you want. This is the theme of our session for today. We are going to look at *signs and symbols*.

page 67

Welcome the Spirit

3. Presentation and activities I

- Distribute the handout on p. 71, 'Signs'.
  Ask the candidates to identify the signs and put them into categories (i.e. information, instruction, warning).
  This exercise can be done individually or in pairs.

- Explain that these are all road signs and that we use a variety of other signs.

- One of the ways in which we communicate is by using our body. The catechist should now give some examples of this and ask the candidates to identify the message which is given: e.g. raising an eyebrow, clenching a fist.

- Distribute the cards from the handout on p. 72 for the 'Body Language' game.
  Each candidate is given one card which has on it a word which, through using their body, they try to communicate to the rest of the group.

- The catechist explains that we reveal something of ourselves through our body.
  Jesus did this.
  Distribute the handout on p. 73, 'Gospel Search'.
  Ask the candidates to identify and explain the body language Jesus used.
  If working with a small group of candidates use at least two stories.
  If working with a larger number of candidates divide them into groups, each with a different story.
  After this take a feedback from the groups.

- Distribute the handout on p. 74, 'Sign or Symbol?'
  Give time for individual candidates to complete the handout and then to share in pairs their ideas.

- The catechist should now ask the candidates to compare the difference between the first handout 'Signs' and the one they have just completed.

- The responses should be written up on large sheets of paper—you should arrive at some statement like this:

    Signs are things which give information, instruction or warnings. They have only one meaning. They do not make us do what they tell us.

    Symbols are things or actions which can represent several ideas. They need to be interpreted in order to be understood. They tell us something about the other person. They invite us to make a response.

4. Refreshment break

5. Presentation and activities II

- Linking the ideas from the first part of the evening's activities, the catechist should say something like this:

    We've seen that people's actions are often symbolic. They tell us what the person feels about us, or wants to do for us; e.g. when someone at home cooks a meal it usually means more than just preparing the food—it actually means 'I love you, I care for you, I look after you'; or another example: if we are upset and someone puts an arm around us it means 'I love you, I care for

you, I want you to feel better'. Even though we don't often appreciate it, we are surrounded by things which tell us about who God is and what God wants to do for us. The very first way in which God is *revealed* is in the *world around us*.

The catechist should give some examples from their own experience of how the created world has revealed God to them in, for instance:

   the power of the sea
   the majesty of the mountains
   the beauty of the sunset.

Ask the candidates if they have had similar experiences.

- The second way in which God *reveals* love and care is through *people*. The catechist should give examples of how someone has revealed to them something of God (ideally, the example should not be a 'churchy' figure—but someone the candidates may more easily identify with, e.g. grandparent, neighbour, brother or sister). Ask the candidates if they have had similar experiences.

- The most important way in which God is *revealed* is in Jesus. The actions of Jesus always tell us:
     firstly—that God loves us
     secondly—of all that God wants to do for us.
  The actions of Jesus are *symbolic* actions.

- Using a large sheet of paper the group/s should brainstorm the actions of Jesus which they can remember. Then they should identify some meaning of these actions, for example,

     Jesus heals the blind man/Jesus wants us to be able to see God.
     Jesus multiplies the loaves/Jesus feeds us.

- The catechist, using the examples given by the candidates and adding to them if necessary, should schematize the actions of Jesus to correspond to the seven sacramental signs:

  1. Jesus wants us to have life (Baptism).
  2. Jesus wants us to become like him (Confirmation).
  3. Jesus wants us to be free and to grow (Reconciliation).
  4. Jesus wants to give us the strength to serve others (Eucharist).
  5. Jesus wants to heal us (Anointing of the Sick).
  6. Jesus wants us to know how to love as a family (Matrimony).
  7. Jesus wants us to live and love as a community (Holy Orders).

(Note that there will be overlap since *all* the sacraments are gifts which help us to grow in the likeness of Jesus.)

To do this Jesus gave us *seven great symbolic actions*: distribute the handout on p. 75, 'Link the Sacrament, the Picture and the Action'. Ask the candidates to see if they can link the sentences, pictures and titles together.

6. Prayer

- Begin by playing quiet music.

- Over the music say:

    Lord Jesus Christ,
    you have come among us
    to show us how to live.
    Help us to live and love like you,
       in our homes,
       in our schools,
       with our friends,
       and with all those we know.
       Amen.

- Reading (John 14):

    Jesus said:
    'If you ask for anything in my name I will do it,
    I shall ask the Father, and he will give you another Advocate,
    to be with you for ever, the Spirit of Truth.
    I will not leave you orphans,
    I will come back to you.
    In a short time the world will no longer see me:
    but you will see me,
    because I live and you will live.
    Anybody who loves me will be loved by my Father and I shall love them and show myself to them.'

- Short pause for silent reflection.

- Say together:

    Day by day,
    three things I pray,
    to see you more clearly,
    love you more dearly,
    and follow you more nearly.

- Hymn, e.g. 'Peace, Perfect Peace'.

7. Conclusion

- Ask the candidates to complete the assignment on the handout on p. 76, 'An Interview' during the week. (Interview someone about their experience of God.)

- Ensure that all candidates put their handouts in their A4 folder.

- Thank the candidates for coming.

Team reflection

1. Did the session go well? Make a note of any adaptations you would recommend for future use.

2. Were there any reflections on the Celebration of Enrolment worth noting?

3. Have any problems emerged? How can they be dealt with?

SIGN AND SYMBOL

SIGNS

This sign tells us
_____
_____

This sign tells us
_____
_____

This sign tells us
_____
_____

This sign tells us
_____
_____

This sign tells us
_____
_____

This sign tells us
_____
_____

This sign tells us
_____
_____

This sign tells us
_____
_____

This sign tells us
_____
_____

These signs make up three different groups

Group 1
This is a group of
signs which
_____
_____
_____

Group 2
This is a group of
signs which
_____
_____
_____

Group 3
This is a group of
signs which
_____
_____
_____

© Sister Mary Bernard Potter SP and Nigel Bavidge 1993.
Multiple copies of this page may be made by the purchasing church or group only.

BODY LANGUAGE

NERVOUS	EAGER
INTERESTED	ANGRY
PANIC STRICKEN	shy
BORED	AMUSED
SULK Y	RELAXED

© Sister Mary Bernard Potter SP and Nigel Bavidge 1993.
Multiple copies of this page may be made by the purchasing church or group only.

SIGN AND SYMBOL

GOSPEL SEARCH

A leper came to him and pleaded on his knees: 'If you want to,' he said, 'you can cure me.' Feeling sorry for him, Jesus stretched out his hand and touched him. 'Of course I want to!' he said. 'Be cured!' And the leprosy left him at once and he was cured.

(Mark 1:40–42)

People were bringing little children to him, for him to touch them. The disciples turned them away, but when Jesus saw this he was indignant and said to them, 'Let the little children come to me; do not stop them; for it is to such as these that the kingdom of God belongs. I tell you solemnly, anyone who does not welcome the kingdom of God like a little child will never enter it.' Then he put his arms round them, laid his hands on them and gave them his blessing.

(Mark 10:13–16)

They were at supper ... Jesus knew that the Father had put everything into his hands, and that he had come from God and was returning to God, and he got up from the table, removed his outer garment and, taking a towel, wrapped it round his waist; he then poured water into a basin and began to wash his disciples' feet and to wipe them with the towel he was wearing.

(John 13:2–5)

Then Jesus came with them to a small estate called Gethsemane; and he said to his disciples, 'Stay here while I go over there to pray.' He took Peter and the two sons of Zebedee with him. And sadness came over him, and great distress. Then he said to them, 'My soul is sorrowful to the point of death. Wait here and keep awake with me.' And going on a little further he fell on his face and prayed, 'My Father,' he said, 'if it is possible, let this cup pass me by. Nevertheless, let it be as you, not I, would have it.'

(Matthew 26:36–39)

© Sister Mary Bernard Potter SP and Nigel Bavidge 1993.
Multiple copies of this page may be made by the purchasing church or group only.

SIGN AND SYMBOL

SIGN OR SYMBOL?

[1] School

S_____

[2]

S_____

[3]

S_____

[4] Bus Lane

S_____

[5]

S_____

[6] 18th Birthday

S_____

Can you now complete these sentences:

A sign is _____

_____

A symbol is _____

_____

© Sister Mary Bernard Potter SP and Nigel Bavidge 1993.
Multiple copies of this page may be made by the purchasing church or group only.

SIGN AND SYMBOL

Link the Sacrament, the Picture and the Action

Sacrament	Picture	Action
BAPTISM	1.	A. Breaking and sharing the bread and the wine and the words: 'This is my body. This is my blood.'
CONFIRMATION	2.	B. Anointing the head and hands and the words: 'Through this holy anointing may the Lord in his love and mercy help you with the grace of the Holy Spirit.'
EUCHARIST	3.	C. The exchange of vows and the words: '... to have and to hold from this day forward.'
RECONCILIATION	4.	D. The pouring of water and the words: 'I baptize you in the name of the Father and of the Son and of the Holy Spirit.'
ANOINTING OF THE SICK	5.	E. The laying on of hands and the words: 'Almighty Father, grant to this servant of yours the dignity of the priesthood.'
HOLY ORDERS	6.	F. The laying on of hands and the words: 'I absolve you from your sins ...'
MATRIMONY	7.	G. The laying on of hands, the anointing and the words: 'N. be sealed with the gift of the Holy Spirit.'

© Sister Mary Bernard Potter SP and Nigel Bavidge 1993.
Multiple copies of this page may be made by the purchasing church or group only.

SIGN AND SYMBOL

AN INTERVIEW

You are an interviewer working for your local radio station. The producer of *Believing*, a religious programme which goes out every Sunday, has asked you to interview some people about their understanding of God. The producer wants you to obtain an example of the way in which someone has felt God to be near them.

By interviewing someone you know, see if you can find a suitable example to use in this programme.

Before you interview anyone you must work out the questions you need to ask to get the information. You should only use three questions.

Question: _____

Answer: _____

_____

_____

_____

_____

Question: _____

Answer: _____

_____

_____

_____

_____

Question: _____

Answer: _____

_____

_____

_____

_____

© Sister Mary Bernard Potter SP and Nigel Bavidge 1993.
Multiple copies of this page may be made by the purchasing church or group only.

Unit 4

ALIVE IN THE SACRAMENTS

UNIT AIMS

1. To deepen the candidates' awareness of the significance of the sacraments.
2. To familiarize the candidates with the sacramental action within the Rite of Confirmation.
3. To explore with the candidates the meaning of the symbolic sacramental action.

OUTLINE

1. Welcome and prayer (*5 mins*)
2. Presentation and activities I (*35 mins*)
3. Refreshment break (*10 mins*)
4. Presentation and activities II (*25 mins*)
5. Prayer (*10 mins*)
6. Conclusion (*5 mins*)

MATERIALS

'The Sacraments' (*handout on p. 82*)
'Can You Remember?' (*handout on p. 83*)
'For Your Eyes Only' (*handout on p. 84*)
Large sheets of paper
Felt-tip pens, pencils and pens
Tape recorder and music
Spare prayer sheets (*handout on p. 35*)
Oil and cotton wool
Hymn books

page 77

Welcome the Spirit

PREPARATION

- Prepare a focal point – title: 'Be sealed with the gift of the Holy Spirit'—incorporating red drape, cut-out cross, small container of oil.
- Refreshments.
- Make sure tape is set correctly.

SESSION

1. Welcome and prayer

- The catechists welcome everyone.
- Using the handout on p. 35, introduce and say the prayer together. This handout should be in the candidates' files, though it may be advisable to have a few spare copies available!

> … pour out your Spirit
> upon your people,
> and grant us
> a new vision of your glory,
> a new experience of your power,
> a new faithfulness to your Word,
> a new consecration to your service,
> that your love may grow among us,
> and your kingdom come;
> through Christ, our Lord.
> Amen.

2. Presentation and activities I

- The catechist introduces the session by reminding the candidates of the major themes of the previous session:
  (a) we are surrounded by *signs* which give us information, instructions or warnings, but these signs do not necessarily make us act in a particular way;
  (b) we are surrounded by *symbols* which need to be interpreted; they tell us what people think or feel; they ask for a response;
  (c) symbols speak to us of God's love and care.

- Invite the candidates to share the assignment on the handout on p. 76, 'An Interview', which was distributed at the previous session.

- The catechist should draw together the ideas which have emerged from the candidates' sharing, saying something like this:

    Lots of people have felt God's presence near them. Some have felt God near because of the kindness of other people, or because of a beautiful sunset, etc.

Unit Four: Alive in the Sacraments

The catechist should, if possible, share a personal experience of this sense of God's presence.

Everything we experience is a symbol of God's presence and can tell us about God if we learn how to recognize and interpret the symbol.

- While everything can speak to us of God, Jesus left us in the Church some symbolic actions (outward signs) which make present God's love and care. The great symbolic actions are called the *sacraments*.

- As a quick recap exercise distribute the handout on p. 82, 'The Sacraments' and ask the candidates to complete the exercise by linking the name of the Sacrament to the symbolic action (outward sign).

- In this section the candidates will be introduced to the signs and symbols which they will experience in the Rite of Confirmation. The ceremony is full of significant signs and symbols and care must be taken to distinguish between the great sacramental action, *the Chrismation*, which includes:
  — laying on of hands
  — anointing with oil of chrism
  — signing with the Cross
  — words: **'N. be sealed with the Holy Spirit'**, together with the response **'Amen'**.

  and the *other symbols* which express aspects of the meaning of the Sacrament:
  — the community
  — the candidates
  — the Bishop (mitre, crozier)
  — the sponsor
  — the Word
  — the Eucharist
  — the laying on of hands and accompanying prayer
  — the renewal of baptismal promises
  — the Peace
  — the visual representations of the Holy Spirit, e.g. red vestments, fire, dove.

- The catechist should introduce this section saying something like this:

  When you are confirmed many things will be said and done, all of which are important. But the most important part will be when you kneel in front of the Bishop and he confers the Sacrament of Confirmation. Let's see how he does this.

  The catechist could now role-play the sacramental action, i.e.
  (a) dip thumb in oil
  (b) place hand on a candidate's head
  (c) trace the cross on candidate's forehead with the thumb, whilst saying:
  (d) 'N. be sealed with the gift of the Holy Spirit.'

- The catechist now asks the candidates if they can identify the four actions which make up the sacramental action. As they are identified write them up on a large sheet of paper:
  — laying on of hands
  — anointing with oil of chrism
  — signing with the Cross
  — words 'N. be sealed ...' together with the response **'Amen'**.

3. Refreshment break

Welcome the Spirit

4. Presentation and activities II

- The catechist should now explore with the candidates the four elements of the sacramental action, the Chrismation.

Laying on of hands

- Explain that we use touch to symbolize lots of different things—a hug, a kiss. Ask the candidates in pairs to show how by using touch they can express the following:
  (a) saying hello
  (b) congratulations
  (c) comforting someone.

- The catechist asks the candidates to imagine that a friend is facing a new and very challenging situation, which is going to require a lot of courage. How would they show their support? Let them act it out.

- The catechist now explains that when the Bishop puts his hand on the candidate's head, he is showing in a symbolic way what God wants to do for us in the Sacrament of Confirmation:
  — encouraging us to live as Jesus taught us, despite the difficulties
  — promising to be with us always, helping us to live as we should
  — giving us the power to live as Christians.

Anointing with oil of chrism

- The catechist explains that oil is a very ancient symbol which has many meanings. The oil of chrism symbolizes three important things:
  (a) consecration (in the Old Testament oil was used to anoint priests, prophets and kings)—in the anointing we are 'set apart'/consecrated for service
  (b) strengthening (oil was/is used by athletes and sportsplayers to tone up muscles before strenuous activity)
  (c) the oil of chrism is olive oil mixed with balsam to give it a sweet smell. This is to represent the 'sweetness' of belonging to Christ.

Signing with the Cross

- The catechist reminds the candidates that a short while ago they signed an important document (at the Celebration of Enrolment). Ask the candidates why they were asked to sign the document—what did it mean? Explain that when we are signed with the Cross we are signed with God's signature.

- Remind the candidates that when they were baptized one of the very first things that happened was that the priest, their parents and godparents traced the sign of the Cross on their foreheads as a sign that they belonged to God. Now in Confirmation God is '*confirming*' that they have been chosen to belong in a special way to God, as members of the Church. The Cross is an emblem/badge of the followers of Christ.

The words 'N. be sealed with the gift of the Holy Spirit' together with the response 'Amen'

- Explain that all that God is promising to do for us is made possible through the power of the Holy Spirit. In Confirmation God signs us and gives us in a new and special way the gift of the presence of the Holy Spirit in our lives. When we answer 'Amen' to the Bishop's words it is a symbol that we are willing to accept the gift which is offered.

5. Prayer

- Begin by playing quiet music.
- Over the music say:

    > Lord Jesus Christ,
    > you have come among us
    > to show us how to live.
    > Help us to live and love like you,
    >   in our homes,
    >   in our schools,
    >   with our friends,
    >   and with all those we know.
    >   Amen.

- Prayer:
  (The leader announces the response: 'Come, Holy Spirit, fill the hearts of your faithful.')

    Leader: Jesus promised to send his Holy Spirit to us and so we pray:
    All: Come, Holy Spirit, fill the hearts of your faithful.
    Leader: Send us your Spirit to help us to live like Jesus.
    All: Come, Holy Spirit, fill the hearts of your faithful.
    Leader: Send us your Spirit to give us strength and courage.
    All: Come, Holy Spirit, fill the hearts of your faithful.
    Leader: Send us your Spirit so that we may know that you are always with us.
    All: Come, Holy Spirit, fill the hearts of your faithful.

- Hymn, e.g. 'Spirit Of The Living God'.

6. Conclusion

- Distribute handout on p. 83, 'Can You Remember?', which summarizes the content of this session, and ask the candidates to complete it before the next session. (This activity may be more suitable for younger candidates.)
- Distribute the handout on p. 84, 'For Your Eyes Only', and ask the candidates to complete it—stress that no one will ask to see it, nor will they be asked to share publicly what they have written on this handout.
- Thank the candidates for coming.

Team reflection

1. Did the session go well? Make a note of any adaptations you would recommend for future use.
2. Have any problems emerged? How can they be dealt with?

ALIVE IN THE SACRAMENTS

The Sacraments

ORDINATION   ANOINTING OF THE SICK   PENANCE

MARRIAGE   EUCHARIST   BAPTISM   CONFIRMATION

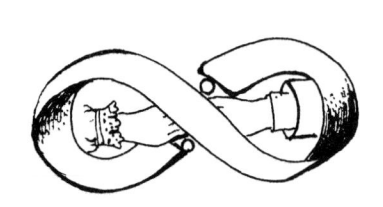

© Sister Mary Bernard Potter SP and Nigel Bavidge 1993.
Multiple copies of this page may be made by the purchasing church or group only.

ALIVE IN THE SACRAMENTS

Can you remember?

God speaks to us in many ways. In the beauty of a sunset, in the power of the sea, in the kindness of people we know.

God also speaks to us in the _____ sacraments, the special _____ of God's _____ and care.

In the Sacrament of Confirmation we are given the special gift of the _____.

Holy Spirit   seven   love   symbols

I will be confirmed by the _____.

The special symbol of Confirmation has _____ parts, they are:

　　the l_____ on of h_____.

　　the a_____ with the oil of c_____.

　　the s_____ with the C_____.

　　the w_____ 'N. be s_____ with the g_____ of the H_____ S_____.'

When the Bishop says the words, I will reply 'A_____.'

Spirit   hands   Holy   chrism   words   signing
Amen   bishop   gift   Cross   four   laying
anointing   sealed

© Sister Mary Bernard Potter sp and Nigel Bavidge 1993.
Multiple copies of this page may be made by the purchasing church or group only.

ALIVE IN THE SACRAMENTS

For your eyes only

When you are confirmed the Bishop will lay his hands on your head as a symbol of God giving you power to live as Jesus taught you.

What do you want God to do for you?

_____
_____
_____
_____
_____

You will be anointed with the oil of chrism as a symbol that God will give you the strength to live as Jesus taught us.

What strength do you need?

_____
_____
_____
_____
_____

Can you write a prayer just for yourself about what you want God to do for you?

_____
_____
_____
_____
_____

© Sister Mary Bernard Potter SP and Nigel Bavidge 1993.
Multiple copies of this page may be made by the purchasing church or group only.

Unit 5

GIFTS OF THE SPIRIT

UNIT AIMS

1. To deepen the candidates' awareness of the role of the Holy Spirit in their lives.
2. Through reflection on the Pentecost story, to explore the power of the Holy Spirit in the Church.
3. To begin to identify the gifts which are guaranteed through the gift of Confirmation.

OUTLINE

1. Welcome and prayer (5 *mins*)
2. Presentation and activities I (20 *mins*) (15 *mins*)
3. Refreshment break (10 *mins*)
4. Presentation and activities II (30 *mins*)
5. Prayer (7 *mins*)
6. Conclusion (3 *mins*)

MATERIALS

'Word Match' (*handout on p. 91*)
'A Command and a Promise' (*handout on p. 92*)
'Pentecost' (*handout on p. 93*)
'A Changed Man' (*handout on p. 94*)
'The Gifts of the Holy Spirit' (*handout on p. 95*)
'Stephen—the First Martyr' (*handout on p. 96*)

Large sheets of paper
Felt-tip pens, pencils and pens
Video equipment and Zeffirelli's *Jesus of Nazareth* (if used)
Bibles
Hymn books

Welcome the Spirit

Preparation

- Prepare a focal point—title: 'Send us your gifts'—surround the caption with the names of the seven gifts of the Holy Spirit. Try to incorporate into the display the symbols of fire and wind.
- Refreshments.
- Video tape, if used, set up correctly.

Session

1. Welcome and prayer

- The catechists welcome everyone.
- Using the handout on p. 35, introduce and say the prayer together. This handout should be in the candidates' files, though it may be advisable to have a few spare copies available!

> … pour out your Spirit
> upon your people,
> and grant us
> a new vision of your glory,
> a new experience of your power,
> a new faithfulness to your Word,
> a new consecration to your service,
> that your love may grow among us,
> and your kingdom come;
> through Christ, our Lord.
> Amen.

2. Presentation and activities 1

- The catechist begins the session by reminding the candidates of the previous session. This could be done through a question and answer session based on the handout on p. 83, 'Can You Remember?', if used, which the candidates were asked to complete.
- The catechist explains that in this session the group are going to look more deeply into the gifts which are given to us at Confirmation (*inward grace*).

The following section may be done in either of two ways:

A role play, which should take place *after* initial discussion with the candidates,

or

A guided scripture meditation. This should only be undertaken with groups of candidates who are able to enter into an extended period of silent reflection and prayer.

Unit Five: Gifts of the Spirit

A role play

- The candidates are asked to imagine that they are a group of the Apostles in the Upper Room, where the Last Supper had been celebrated.

  It is the evening of Good Friday.
  — what are they feeling?
  — what are they remembering?
  — what are they saying?

  The candidates could act out this scene. When they have completed this exercise the catechist should draw out, through discussion, a list which identifies the feelings which the apostles had at this time. This list should be written up on a large sheet of paper.

A guided scripture meditation

- The catechist should paint a 'word picture' of this scene, e.g. invite the candidates to close their eyes and picture the Upper Room, where Jesus a few hours earlier had celebrated the Last Supper. The room is quite dark, two or three little oil lamps flicker; even in the gloom you can make out the Apostles' faces. They look tired and worn out. They talk quietly among themselves, sometimes finding it hard to speak. Some of them are near to tears. There is a sudden noise in the street outside— immediately they stop talking and look anxiously at the door. Very quietly one gets up and goes noiselessly to check the bolts on the door. Everyone is very tense.
  — what are they feeling?
  — what are they remembering?
  — what are they saying?

  List the responses on a large sheet of paper.

- The catechist should briefly tell the story of the events which lead from Good Friday to Pentecost Day:

  > On the night of Good Friday the Apostles must have felt a painful sense of loss. It was not just that they had lost a friend through death, but the death that Jesus had suffered was long and cruel, and above all it was unjust.
  >
  > The Apostles had hoped that Jesus would have been the one to set the people free—only a week earlier, on Palm Sunday, it seemed possible that Jesus could have led a rebellion against the hated Romans. Much as they admired him and loved him, he seemed to have let them down. But they too had let him down. One of their friends, Judas, had betrayed him, but then hadn't they all? Only John had had the courage to stay close to Jesus throughout the terrible events of Thursday night and Friday. Perhaps none felt it more than Peter who had boasted that he would never leave Jesus. Friday night, Saturday and Sunday were a nightmare! They were terrified that the Jewish authorities would come for them and that they would suffer the same fate as Jesus.
  >
  > On Sunday morning, their confusion and bewilderment increased. Some of the women who were followers of Jesus had returned from the tomb where Jesus had been buried, saying that it was empty and that they had been told in a vision that Jesus had risen from the dead.
  >
  > On Sunday evening nearly all the Apostles were together in the Upper Room when Jesus appeared to them. Now they knew that the women had been right—Jesus had indeed risen from the dead. During the next forty days Jesus

Welcome the Spirit

often appeared to his friends. He reminded them of all the things he had said and done and he prepared them for their mission in the world.

Forty days after the Resurrection Jesus took his friends to a hill top outside Jerusalem. This was the last time they saw him. He gave them his last instructions and then he was taken from their sight.

(If you have video equipment, this period in the life of Jesus is well represented in the last part of Zeffirelli's Jesus of Nazareth.)

- Distribute the handout on p. 91, 'Word Match', and ask the candidates, working in pairs, to complete it.

3. Refreshment break

4. Presentation and activities II

- In order to make the link with the ideas explored earlier, distribute the handout on p. 92, 'A Command and a Promise', and ask the candidates to complete it.

- The catechist continues telling the story linking Ascension Day to Pentecost, saying something like this:

    We saw that, on the day of the Ascension, Jesus instructed his friends to go and proclaim the Good News throughout the world (Matthew 28), to help others to become disciples and bring them to membership of the Church through Baptism. Jesus knew, however, that before they would be ready to undertake this important *mission* they needed a special *power*. The apostles didn't have the understanding or the courage to do this by themselves.

    When Jesus had returned to his Father the Apostles did as he had told them and returned to the city. Once more they felt lost and afraid. While Jesus had been with them they had had confidence. Now they were not sure what to do.

    For ten days they hid in the Upper Room. Then on Pentecost Day, ten days after the Ascension and fifty days after the Day of Resurrection, the Apostles had an experience which not only changed them, but changed the whole history of the world.

- Distribute the handout on p. 93, 'Pentecost', and read through the text with the candidates.

- Explore with the candidates the two great symbols of the Holy Spirit (i.e. fire and wind). They are things which can be experienced, but not grasped or contained.

- Examine other symbolic meanings of

Fire	**Wind**
warming	power
destroying	destructive
purifying	cooling
life-giving	refreshing
enthusiasm	disturbing
power	

- Discuss with the candidates why these two symbols should be used in connection with the Holy Spirit. Draw up with the candidates a list of sentences similar to these:

    The Holy Spirit is the One who gives us enthusiasm.

Unit Five: Gifts of the Spirit

> The Holy Spirit is the One who purifies our hearts and minds.
> The Holy Spirit is the One who destroys what is evil in us.
> The Holy Spirit is the One who disturbs our complacency.
> The Holy Spirit is the One who refreshes us, etc.

- Distribute the handout on p. 94, 'A Changed Man'. Ask the candidates to complete it, working in pairs.

- Discuss with the candidates the answers they have given on the handout.

- The catechist now formally introduces the *seven gifts* of the *Holy Spirit*, saying something like this:

    > As the Apostles began to fulfil Jesus' instruction that they should preach the Good News and help people to become disciples of Jesus, they began to realize that the Holy Spirit, whom Jesus had promised the Father would send, had indeed come to them and brought them great gifts.

- Distribute the handout on p. 95, 'The Gifts of the Holy Spirit'. Explain briefly what each gift is:

    Wisdom – to help us judge in the way God does.
    Understanding – to help us to understand all that God has told us.
    Right Judgement – to help us to know what to do, especially in difficult situations.
    Courage – to give us the strength to do what is right no matter how hard this may be.
    Knowledge – to let us see the world as it really is.
    Reverence – to give us the power to love God and each other as we should.
    Awe and Wonder – to give us the power to remember and appreciate the greatness of God and to help us to want to love God and to reject sin.

5. Prayer

- Hymn to the Holy Spirit, e.g. 'Spirit Of The Living God'.

- Reading (John 14:16):
    > Jesus said
    > 'I shall ask the Father,
    > and he will give you another Advocate
    > to be with you for ever.'

- Invitation to silence:
    > Let's pray in the silence of our hearts that God will send the Holy Spirit to fill us with the promised gifts. Perhaps there is one gift you feel you need very specially.

- Say together:
    > Day by day,
    > three things I pray,
    > to see you more clearly,
    > love you more dearly,
    > and follow you more nearly.

- Blessing by catechist:
   > May God bless you and keep you.
   > May God send you the Holy Spirit
   > and make you courageous followers
   > of Jesus Christ, our Lord.
   > All: Amen.

6. Conclusion

- Distribute the handout on p. 96, 'Stephen—the First Martyr', and ask the candidates to complete it ready for the next session.
- Ensure that all candidates put their handouts in their A4 folder.
- Thank the candidates for coming.

Team reflection

1. Did the session go well? Make a note of any adaptations you would recommend for future use.
2. Have any problems emerged? How can they be dealt with?

GIFTS OF THE SPIRIT

WORD MATCH

Good Friday

– – – – – – – – – – – **3 days** – – – – – – – – – – –

Easter Day

– – – – – – – – – – – **40 days** – – – – – – – – – – –

Ascension Day

Where on this chart would you put these words? *(There are eight for each section)*
END HOPE WONDER LEAVING SORROW DEATH JOY
AMAZEMENT PROMISE SHAME LIFE COMMAND
MISSION GUILT DESPAIR WAITING RESURRECTION
GLORY CONFUSION BEGINNING GLOOM EXPECTATION
PEACE QUESTION

© Sister Mary Bernard Potter SP and Nigel Bavidge 1993.
Multiple copies of this page may be made by the purchasing church or group only.

GIFTS OF THE SPIRIT

A COMMAND AND A PROMISE

God goes up with shouts of joy. The Lord ascends with trumpet blasts.

Before Jesus ascended into heaven he gave a final command which was? (Look at St Matthew's Gospel, chapter 28)

The command was in four parts. What were they?

1. _____

2. _____

3. _____

4. _____

Jesus also made a great promise. What was it?

The promise was _____

_____

_____

Much earlier, at the Last Supper, Jesus had promised that when he returned to God, he would ask for a gift to be sent to his friends.

What did Jesus promise? (Look at St John's Gospel, chapter 14)

_____

_____

_____

© Sister Mary Bernard Potter SP and Nigel Bavidge 1993.
Multiple copies of this page may be made by the purchasing church or group only.

GIFTS OF THE SPIRIT

PENTECOST

When Pentecost day came round, they had all met in one room, when suddenly they heard what sounded like a powerful wind from heaven, the noise of which filled the entire house in which they were sitting; and something appeared to them that seemed like tongues of fire; these separated and came to rest on the head of each of them. They were all filled with the Holy Spirit, and began to speak in foreign languages as the Spirit gave them the gift of speech.

Now there were devout men living in Jerusalem from every nation under heaven, and at this sound they all assembled, each one bewildered to hear these men speaking his own language. They were amazed and astonished. 'Surely,' they said, 'all these men speaking are Galileans? How does it happen that each of us hears them in his own native language? Parthians, Medes and Elamites; people from Mesopotamia, Judaea and Cappadocia, Pontus and Asia, Phrygia and Pamphylia, Egypt and the parts of Libya round Cyrene; as well as visitors from Rome—Jews and proselytes alike—Cretans and Arabs; we hear them preaching in our own language about the marvels of God.' Everyone was amazed and unable to explain it; they asked one another what it all meant.

(Acts of the Apostles 2:1–13)

© Sister Mary Bernard Potter SP and Nigel Bavidge 1993.
Multiple copies of this page may be made by the purchasing church or group only.

GIFTS OF THE SPIRIT

A CHANGED MAN

Then Peter stood up with the other eleven apostles and in a loud voice began to speak to the crowd. 'Fellow Jews, and all of you who live in Jerusalem, listen to me and let me tell you what this means . . . this is what the prophet, Joel, spoke about:

God says:
I will pour out my Spirit on everyone.
Your sons and daughters shall proclaim my message.

'Listen to these words! Jesus of Nazareth was a man whose divine authority was clearly proven to you by all the miracles and wonders which God performed through him. This Jesus you handed over to be crucified. But God raised him from death, setting him free from its power. God has raised this very Jesus from death and we are all witnesses to this fact. What you now see and hear is his gift of the Holy Spirit that he has poured out on us. All the people of Israel, then, are to know for sure that this Jesus, whom you crucified, is the one that God has made Lord and Messiah!'

When the people heard this, they were deeply troubled and said to Peter and the other apostles, 'What shall we do?'

Peter said to them, 'Each of you must turn away from sin and be baptized in the name of Jesus Christ and you shall receive the gift of the Holy Spirit.'

(Acts of the Apostles 2)

COLUMN 1 　　　　　　　　COLUMN 2

In which column would you put these words to describe Peter?

Strong　　*Weak*　　*Sure*　　*Courageous*　　*Bewildered*
Confident　　*Afraid*　　*Powerful*　　*Hiding*　　*Fearful*　　*Leader*

© Sister Mary Bernard Potter SP and Nigel Bavidge 1993.
Multiple copies of this page may be made by the purchasing church or group only.

The Gifts of the Holy Spirit

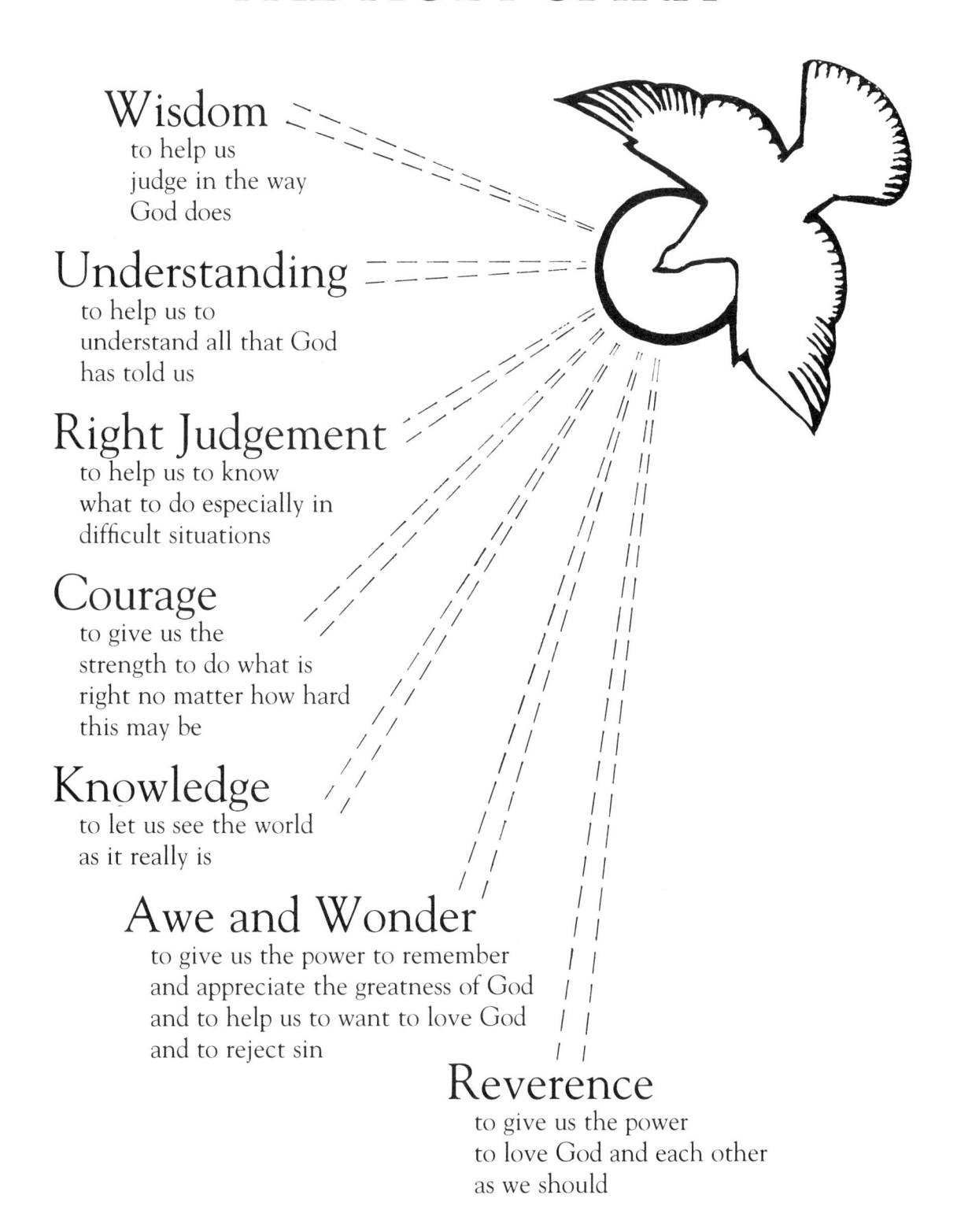

Wisdom
to help us judge in the way God does

Understanding
to help us to understand all that God has told us

Right Judgement
to help us to know what to do especially in difficult situations

Courage
to give us the strength to do what is right no matter how hard this may be

Knowledge
to let us see the world as it really is

Awe and Wonder
to give us the power to remember and appreciate the greatness of God and to help us to want to love God and to reject sin

Reverence
to give us the power to love God and each other as we should

© Sister Mary Bernard Potter SP and Nigel Bavidge 1993.
Multiple copies of this page may be made by the purchasing church or group only.

Stephen—The First Martyr

Stephen, a man richly blessed by God and full of power, performed great miracles and wonders among the people. But he was opposed by some who started arguing with him. But the Spirit gave Stephen such wisdom that when he spoke, they could not refute him. So they bribed some men to say, 'We heard him speaking against Moses and against God!' In this way they stirred up the people, the elders and the teachers of the Law.

They seized Stephen and took him before the Council.

The High Priest asked Stephen, 'Is all this true?'

'How stubborn you are!' Stephen said. 'How heathen your hearts, how deaf you are to God's message! You are just like your ancestors: you too have always resisted the Holy Spirit! Was there any prophet that your ancestors did not persecute? They killed God's messengers, who long ago announced the coming of his righteous Servant. And now you have betrayed and murdered him. You are the ones who received God's law, that was handed down by angels—yet you have not obeyed it!' As the members of the Council listened to Stephen, they became furious and ground their teeth at him in anger. But Stephen, full of the Holy Spirit, looked up to heaven and saw God's glory and Jesus standing at the right-hand side of God. 'Look!' he said, 'I see heaven opened and the Son of Man standing at the right-hand side of God!'

With a loud cry the members of the Council covered their ears with their hands. Then they all rushed at him at once, threw him out of the city, and stoned him. They kept stoning Stephen as he called out to the Lord, 'Lord Jesus, receive my Spirit!' He knelt down and cried out in a loud voice, 'Lord! Do not remember this sin against them!' He said this and died.

(Acts of the Apostles 6 and 7)

Stephen was a man filled with the Holy Spirit. His life and death showed the power of the Holy Spirit working in him. He showed the gifts of the Holy Spirit.

Stephen showed the gift of _____ when he spoke out fearlessly.

Stephen showed the gift of _____ when he preached the truth about God and the message of Jesus.

Stephen, faced with the difficult choice between life and the love of God, showed the gift of _____.

Stephen showed the gift of _____ when he forgave his executioners, even then he still loved them.

Stephen showed the gift of _____ when he was prepared to die rather than give in to the pressure of the authorities. For Stephen, loving God, even though it cost him his life, was the most important thing.

Stephen showed the gift of _____ when, seeing through God's eyes, he said that what the authorities had done to Jesus was wrong.

Stephen showed the gift of _____ when he saw that life in this world was not as important as life in the world to come.

© Sister Mary Bernard Potter SP and Nigel Bavidge 1993.
Multiple copies of this page may be made by the purchasing church or group only.

Unit 6

YOU WILL BE MY WITNESSES

UNIT AIMS

1. To explore the evidence of the power of the Spirit in the lives of Christians.
2. To identify ways in which the candidates may have to respond to the demands of Christian living.
3. To examine the vocation and mission to which Confirmation calls us.

OUTLINE

1. Welcome and prayer (*5 mins*)
2. Presentation and activities I (*30 mins*)
3. Refreshment break (*10 mins*)
4. Presentation and activities II (*25 mins*)
5. Presentation and activities III (*10 mins*)
6. Prayer (*5 mins*)
7. Conclusion (*5 mins*)

MATERIALS

'The Gifts Today' (*handout on pp. 102–103*)
'Wordsearch' (*handout on p. 104*)
'Prayer of St Francis' (*handout on p. 105*)

'Living the Prayer' (*handout on p. 106*)
Large sheets of paper
Felt-tip pens, pencils and pens
Hymn books

page 97

Welcome the Spirit

PREPARATION

- Prepare a focal point—title: 'Gifts to change our world'. Surround the caption with newspaper cuttings of war, violence, inner-city decay, etc. Superimpose words (taken from prayer of St Francis, e.g. joy, peace, forgiveness) over the cuttings.
- Refreshments.
- Tape recorder and quiet music if used during the prayer service.

SESSION

1. Welcome and prayer

- The catechists welcome everyone.
- Using the handout on p. 35, introduce and say the prayer together. This handout should be in the candidates' files, though it may be advisable to have a few spare copies available!

> ... pour out your Spirit
> upon your people,
> and grant us
> a new vision of your glory,
> a new experience of your power,
> a new faithfulness to your Word,
> a new consecration to your service,
> that your love may grow among us,
> and your kingdom come;
> through Christ, our Lord.
> Amen.

[Handwritten margin notes: Why do we say this prayer. This weekend we have the celebration of election. It marks the end of your preparation for the Sacrament. This is not an end it is a beginning – hence the use of the word "new" – new vision etc]

2. Presentation and activities I

- The catechist reminds the candidates that in the last session they had looked at the gifts of the Holy Spirit. Using the completed handout on p. 96, 'Stephen—the First Martyr', list again on large sheets of paper the seven gifts and identify the ways in which these gifts were evident in Stephen. Candidates may come up with a variety of answers, all of which should be accepted, since there is a great deal of overlap between the gifts of the Holy Spirit. Our suggested order is: courage, understanding, right judgement, reverence, awe and wonder, wisdom and knowledge.

- The catechist explains that throughout the centuries there have been many examples of men and women and young people who have shown in very powerful ways the presence of the Holy Spirit in their lives, such as:
    Maximilian Kolbe
    Oscar Romero
    Edwina Gateley (foundress of Volunteer Missionary Movement)
    Margaret Clitherow

[Handwritten margin note: We are going to talk about what we are beginning when we are Confirmed]

Unit Six: You will be my Witnesses

Mother Teresa
Garvan Byrne (a videotaped interview with Garvan who died, aged 11, is available)

- The catechist should point out that it is not only those who are famous who show the power of the Spirit in their lives. These gifts are present in many people's lives in a variety of ways. Distribute the handout on pp. 102–103, 'The Gifts Today', and ask the candidates, working in pairs, to complete it. When completed, draw together the findings.

- Ask the candidates to work in groups of three or four to prepare a short role-play/ sketch to show how they might be called upon to use the gifts of the Holy Spirit in their everyday lives. These sketches can then be presented to the whole group.

3. Refreshment break

4. Presentation and activities II

- The catechist explains that in Confirmation we are given *gifts* which are not just for ourselves, but are for others. Through Confirmation we are called in a special way by God to live more like Jesus and to share in the work of Jesus today in our world. We were first called to this in Baptism. Through Confirmation we are given all the strength and all the gifts necessary to do what God asks of us.

- Confirmation is a *call from God* to share in the work of Jesus. This call from God is called a *vocation* and the work we are asked to do is our *mission*.

- We were first called to this vocation and mission when we were baptized. During our baptismal ceremony we were anointed to share in Jesus' vocation and ministry.

- Distribute the handout on p. 104, 'Wordsearch', and ask the candidates to complete it. (This activity may be more suitable for younger candidates.)

- Introducing the prayer of St Francis, the catechist should explain that the mission to which we have been called is to bring love, justice and peace into the world. St Francis understood this and his prayer reminds us that it is into the ordinary everyday events that we are to bring these values. Distribute the handout on p. 105, 'Prayer of St Francis', and ask the candidates, working in pairs, to take one line of the prayer and prepare a two-minute presentation on how we can live this section of the prayer in our everyday lives.

- The candidates now share their two-minute presentation with the whole group.

5. Presentation and activities III

- The catechist should now prepare the candidates for the Celebration of Election.

- The candidates should be reminded that when they chose to be part of the Preparation Programme for Confirmation they took part in the Celebration of Enrolment. It should now be explained that since they have had time to reflect on the gifts and responsibilities of Confirmation, they must now make their choice to receive the Sacrament of Confirmation.

- The decision to be confirmed will be affirmed in the Celebration of Election, during which their catechists will testify to their sincerity and the parish community will offer their prayerful support.

Welcome the Spirit

- The catechist should explain the structure of the Celebration of Election and give details of the time and place.

6. Prayer

- Hymn, e.g. 'God's Spirit Is In My Heart' *or* 'When I Needed A Neighbour'.
- Reading (John 13:34–35):
    Jesus said
    'I give you a new commandment:
    Love one another; just as I have loved you,
    you also must love one another.
    By this love you have for one another,
    everyone will know that you are my
    disciples.'
- Invitation to silence:
    Let's pray in the silence of our hearts that through the gifts of the Holy Spirit, which will be given to us in Confirmation, we might bring joy, happiness and peace to our families, our friends and all our world.
- Say the prayer of St Francis (this could be said either by one person or each line could be said by a different person).

    Then say together:
    Day by day,
    three things I pray,
    to see you more clearly,
    love you more dearly,
    and follow you more nearly.

- Blessing by catechist:
    May God bless you and keep you.
    May God send you the Holy Spirit
    to fill you with the gifts
    to make our world a better place.
    All: Amen.

7. Conclusion

- Distribute the handout on p. 106, 'Living the Prayer'. Explain to the candidates how to use the handout, but stress that they will not be asked to share publicly what they write on it.
- Ensure that all candidates put their handouts in their A4 folders.
- Remind the candidates of the arrangements for the Celebration of Election.
- Remind the candidates to bring the completed handout on pp. 56–57, 'I Have Called You by Name', which was distributed at the end of Unit Two, 'Belonging', to the next session.
- Thank the candidates for coming.

Team reflection

1. Did the session go well? Make a note of any adaptations you would recommend for future use.

2. Have any problems emerged? How can they be dealt with?

YOU WILL BE MY WITNESSES

THE GIFTS TODAY

Tracy went with some friends from school on the pilgrimage to Lourdes. There she met Kirsty, who has cerebral palsy. They are now good friends and often on Saturday they go into town together.

What gifts is Tracy using? _____

What gifts is Kirsty using? _____

John and Andy saw on a TV programme how important trees are in helping not just to make the environment to look nice, but also in cleaning up the atmosphere. They talked to their form teacher about this and have formed a tree-planting group in school. So far they have planted fifteen trees round the perimeter of the sports field.

What gifts are John and Andy using? _____

Did their form teacher use any gifts? _____

What about the rest of the class? _____

Mr Richards is 69 and not in very good health. His wife died three years ago. Often he gets very lonely. Mike, his grandson, tries to call in every day on his way home from school to see him. They usually have a good laugh. Mr Richards is great at telling stories.

What gifts is Mr Richards using? _____

What gifts is Mike using? _____

Sue Fallon belongs to a group of voluntary workers in Ethiopia. When she was last home on leave she went to the school to talk about her work. She told them about a young man who was training for nursing, but had to stop his education because his family could no longer afford the fees. Maria and Peter thought they ought to do something about this. With their friends they organized a lot of fund-raising activities. As a result the young man has been able to take up his studies again and will qualify in six months' time.

What gifts is Sue Fallon using? _____

What gifts is the young man using? _____

What gifts are Maria and Peter using? _____

What gifts are their friends using? _____

© Sister Mary Bernard Potter SP and Nigel Bavidge 1993.
Multiple copies of this page may be made by the purchasing church or group only.

THE GIFTS TODAY (CONTINUED)

Joanne's Mum is ill. Joanne has to do a lot of work at home looking after her two sisters. She has become withdrawn and moody. Her school work has slipped; she won't talk to her form teacher, but she can talk to Becky, her friend.

One day, a teacher tells Joanne off in front of the class for not having an assignment ready on time. Joanne just cries and doesn't try to give any explanation. Becky stays behind at the end of the class and explains to the teacher what is going on in Joanne's family. Even though Becky is afraid that Joanne might be annoyed, she realizes she needs help and understanding.

What gifts is Becky using? _____

What gifts is Joanne using? _____

Matthew was looking for a part-time job. Anything would do provided that it put enough money into his pocket. Every evening he carefully read the jobs column in the local paper. There wasn't much work available which fitted into his free time. He was getting desperate. Then one evening he saw an ad for domestic help in a home for elderly people. The job was to serve evening and weekend meals, clear up, and do the washing up. Not much of a job, he thought, but the pay was reasonable and the hours suited him. Some of his friends tried to put him off taking the job – who would want to spend any time with doddery old folk? Matthew was nearly put off the idea, but the thought of the money appealed.

It took time to settle to the job – the job was easy enough, but soon Matthew found he loved talking to the residents and often when he'd finished work he'd stay on just chatting with them, telling them his news and listening to their stories.

What did Matthew discover about himself? _____

What did Matthew discover about the residents? _____

What gifts are being used? _____

© Sister Mary Bernard Potter SP and Nigel Bavidge 1993.
Multiple copies of this page may be made by the purchasing church or group only.

YOU WILL BE MY WITNESSES

WORDSEARCH

Fill in the missing words and then find them in the Wordsearch.

A call from God is a _____

God's call is a call to _____

We first received God's call in the Sacrament of
_____

In the Sacrament of _____ we are strengthened to do what God asks.

In this sacrament we are given the gift of the _____ _____ who brings to us _____ gifts.

B	A	T	Q	U	I	O	N	C	W	H	S
E	M	L	U	J	P	O	K	C	A	E	Z
S	I	T	H	O	I	E	M	F	C	A	L
R	S	O	Y	T	S	E	V	E	N	L	M
I	S	N	A	G	P	S	Q	U	A	S	O
W	I	C	H	F	I	A	M	N	I	H	O
C	O	N	F	I	R	M	A	T	I	O	N
V	N	D	E	P	I	A	P	Y	S	L	B
D	G	H	T	P	T	A	O	K	J	Y	R
R	U	Y	O	M	B	X	I	O	N	T	E

© Sister Mary Bernard Potter SP and Nigel Bavidge 1993.
Multiple copies of this page may be made by the purchasing church or group only.

Prayer of St Francis

Lord, make me an instrument of your peace:
   where there is hatred let me sow love,
   where there is injury let me sow pardon,
   where there is doubt let me sow faith,
   where there is despair let me give hope,
   where there is darkness let me give light,
   where there is sadness let me give joy.

1. Which line are you going to look at?

2. What is the *negative* word in your line? _____

3. Where do you see the effects of this *negative* word in

    (a) your everyday life? _____

    (b) in our country? _____

    (c) in our world? _____

4. What is the *positive* word in your line? _____

5. How can you bring this *positive* word into the examples you gave as answers to question 3?

6. Using the ideas from this sheet prepare a two-minute talk about this line and present your talk to the rest of the group.

© Sister Mary Bernard Potter SP and Nigel Bavidge 1993.
Multiple copies of this page may be made by the purchasing church or group only.

LIVING THE PRAYER

Lord, make me an instrument of your peace:
where there is hatred let me sow love,
where there is injury let me sow pardon,
where there is doubt let me sow faith,
where there is despair let me give hope,
where there is darkness let me give light,
where there is sadness let me give joy.

Each night during the next week fill in this diary and make a note of any way in which you put the prayer of St Francis into practice.

Here's an example:

Today I brought *joy* where there was *sadness* by *cheering up a friend who was fed up.*

DAY 1
Today I brought ———————— by ———————— where there was ————————————————

DAY 2
Today I brought ———————— by ———————— where there was ————————————————

DAY 3
Today I brought ———————— by ———————— where there was ————————————————

DAY 4
Today I brought ———————— by ———————— where there was ————————————————

DAY 5
Today I brought ———————— by ———————— where there was ————————————————

DAY 6
Today I brought ———————— by ———————— where there was ————————————————

DAY 7
Today I brought ———————— by ———————— where there was ————————————————

WELL DONE!!

© Sister Mary Bernard Potter sp and Nigel Bavidge 1993.
Multiple copies of these pages may be made by the purchasing church or group only.

Celebration of Election

Celebration Aims

This celebration is an important part of the preparation of the Confirmation candidates.

Its purposes are:

1. To emphasize the importance of asking to receive a sacrament.

2. To highlight that sacraments are gifts which belong to the Church and that to receive them is a privilege.

3. To deepen the candidates' sense of community and to deepen the parish's awareness of relationship and responsibility to those who are drawn more deeply into the sacramental life of the Church.

Outline

This celebration should take place just before the final blessing during one particular Sunday Eucharist in the parish or at the Sunday Eucharist which the candidates normally attend.

This ceremony is based on the Rite of Election contained in the Rite of Christian Initiation of Adults.

A sample text for the Celebration is given in this section and on the handout on pp. 112–115. See p. 58 for a guide to photocopying the handout.

STRUCTURE

- Presentation of the candidates
- Affirmation
- Election
- Blessing

MATERIALS

Copies of the Celebration of Election for everyone.

THE CELEBRATION OF ELECTION OF CANDIDATES FOR THE SACRAMENT OF CONFIRMATION

Presentation of the Candidates

One of the catechists addresses the priest.

Catechist: Reverend Father,
The Bishop will soon be celebrating the Sacrament of Confirmation and I now present to you these young people who ask that they should receive the gift of the Holy Spirit in the Sacrament of Confirmation. I present to you N. . . .

The catechist reads the names of the candidates, who should stand as their names are called.

Affirmation

The priest addresses the catechist.

Priest: In the name of this community you have worked (with other catechists) in preparing these young people for the Sacrament of Confirmation. I now ask you:

Have they understood the importance of what they are doing?

Catechist: They have.

Priest: Have they taken part conscientiously in the preparation programme?

Catechist: They have.

Priest: Do you believe that they sincerely wish to receive the gift of the Holy Spirit in the Sacrament of Confirmation?

Catechist: I do.

Priest: Let us bless the Lord.

Catechist: Thanks be to God.

The priest now addresses the candidates.

Priest: My dear young people, to ask for the Sacrament of Confirmation is a serious matter.

To be a confirmed member of the Church brings the responsibility of witnessing to Christ and trying to live every day as a true and loyal follower of the Lord.

Welcome the Spirit

Priest:	This is a challenge which will bring great joy and peace. It is a call which requires great courage, strength and love.
	I must, therefore, ask you:
	Do you sincerely want to receive the Sacrament of Confirmation?
Candidates:	I do.
Priest:	Do you understand that through this sacrament God is calling you to become witnesses to Christ?
Candidates:	I do.
Priest:	Do you want to follow the Lord Jesus by living lives of loving service to God and to all God's people?
Candidates:	I do.
Priest:	Let us bless the Lord.
Candidates:	Thanks be to God.

The priest now addresses the whole community.

Priest:	Is it your wish that these young people should be presented to the Bishop for Confirmation?
Congregation:	It is.
Priest:	Are you prepared to support these young people by your witness and by your prayers?
Congregation:	We are.
Priest:	Let us bless the Lord.
Congregation:	Thanks be to God.

Election

The priest again addresses the candidates.

Priest:	Candidates for Confirmation, you have asked to be confirmed and your catechist(s) have spoken on your behalf.
	In the name of God and of this community I declare that God is calling you to receive the gift of the Holy Spirit in the Sacrament of Confirmation.
	Let us bless the Lord.
All:	Thanks be to God.

Blessing

Priest: The God of light enlightened the minds of the disciples by the outpouring of the Holy Spirit.
May God bless you and give you the gifts of the Spirit for ever.

All: Amen.

Priest: May that fire which hovered over the disciples as tongues of flame burn out all evil from your hearts and make them glow with pure light.

All: Amen.

Priest: God inspired speech in different tongues to proclaim one faith. May your faith be strengthened and your hope of seeing God face to face be fulfilled.

All: Amen.

Priest: May almighty God bless you,
the Father, and the Son ✠ and the Holy Spirit.

All: Amen.

Parish of _____

CELEBRATION OF ELECTION OF CANDIDATES FOR CONFIRMATION

Date _____

CANDIDATES' NAMES

© Sister Mary Bernard Potter SP and Nigel Bavidge 1993.
Multiple copies of these pages may be made by the purchasing church or group only.

This Celebration of Election is an important part of the parish preparation of the candidates for the Sacrament of Confirmation.

The purposes of the Celebration are:

- to emphasize the importance of asking to receive a sacrament
- to highlight that sacraments are gifts which belong to the Church and that to receive them is a privilege
- to deepen the candidates' sense of community and to deepen the parish's awareness of relationship and responsibility to those who are drawn more deeply into the sacramental life of the Church.

CELEBRATION OF ELECTION

Presentation of the Candidates

One of the catechists addresses the priest.

Catechist: Reverend Father,
The Bishop will soon be celebrating the Sacrament of Confirmation and I now present to you these young people who ask that they should receive the gift of the Holy Spirit in the Sacrament of Confirmation. I present to you N. . . . .

The catechist reads the names of the candidates, who should stand as their names are called.

Affirmation

The priest addresses the catechist.

Priest: In the name of this community you have worked (with other catechists) in preparing these young people for the Sacrament of Confirmation. I now ask you:

Have they understood the importance of what they are doing?

Catechist: They have.

Priest: Have they taken part conscientiously in the preparation programme?

Catechist: They have.

Priest: May that fire which hovered over the disciples as tongues of flame burn out all evil from your hearts and make them glow with pure light.

All: Amen.

Priest: God inspired speech in different tongues to proclaim one faith.
May your faith be strengthened and may your hope of seeing God face to face be fulfilled.

All: Amen.

Priest: May almighty God bless you, the Father, and the Son ✠ and the Holy Spirit.

All: Amen.

Priest:	Do you believe that they sincerely wish to receive the gift of the Holy Spirit in the Sacrament of Confirmation?
Catechist:	I do.
Priest:	Let us bless the Lord.
Catechist:	Thanks be to God.

The priest now addresses the candidates.

	My dear young people, to ask for the Sacrament of Confirmation is a serious matter.
	To be a confirmed member of the Church brings the responsibility of witnessing to Christ and trying to live every day as a true and loyal follower of the Lord.
	This is a challenge which will bring great joy and peace. It is a call which requires great courage, strength and love.
	I must, therefore, ask you: Do you sincerely want to receive the Sacrament of Confirmation?
Candidates:	I do.
Priest:	Do you understand that through this sacrament God is calling you to become witnesses to Christ?
Candidates:	I do.
Priest:	Do you want to follow the Lord Jesus by living lives of loving service to God and to all God's people?
Candidates:	I do.
Priest:	Let us bless the Lord.
Candidates:	Thanks be to God.

The priest now addresses the whole community.

Priest:	Is it your wish that these young people should be presented to the Bishop for Confirmation?
Congregation:	It is.
Priest:	Are you prepared to support these young people by your witness and by your prayers?
Congregation:	We are.
Priest:	Let us bless the Lord.
Congregation:	Thanks be to God.

Election

The priest again addresses the candidates.

Priest:	Candidates for Confirmation, you have asked to be confirmed and your catechist(s) have spoken on your behalf.
	In the name of God and of this community I declare that God is calling you to receive the gift of the Holy Spirit in the Sacrament of Confirmation.
	Let us bless the Lord.
All:	Thanks be to God.

Blessing

Priest:	The God of light enlightened the minds of the disciples by the outpouring of the Holy Spirit. May God bless you and give you the gifts of the Spirit for ever.
All:	Amen.

Unit 7

Preparing to Celebrate

Unit Aims

1. To familiarize candidates with the structure of the Rite of Confirmation.
2. To examine the elements of the Rite and to explore some of the meanings of these elements.
3. To prepare the candidates for the celebration of the Sacrament of Confirmation.

Outline

1. Welcome and prayer (*5 mins*)
2. Reflection on the Celebration of Election (*10 mins*)
3. Presentation and activities I (*30 mins*)
4. Refreshment break (*15 mins*)
5. Presentation and activities II (*30 mins*)
6. Prayer (*5 mins*)
7. Conclusion (*5 mins*)

Materials

'Celebrating' (*handout on pp. 123–124 or p. 125*)

'Special Occasions' (*handouts on pp. 126–130*)

'Put It in Order' (*handout on p. 131*)

'A Day at a Time' (*handout on pp. 132–133*)

Felt-tip pens, pencils and pens

Large sheets of paper

Hymn books

Slides and tape if being used

Slide projector and screen

Extension cable

Tape recorder

Preparation

In this Unit it is suggested that there should be a slide presentation of the structure of the Celebration of Confirmation.

Your Diocesan RE Centre may be able to provide you with appropriate slides to illustrate the text which is given in this Unit. However, it is recommended that each parish aims eventually to produce a set of slides taken in their own parish church, with their own community. This would help to make the presentation more relevant to the candidates.

The text for a taped commentary is given in this Unit, though there is no reason why the text should not be read or adapted. The advantage of a taped commentary is that it is easier for the catechist to use.

- Ensure that the tape is correctly set and the slide projector is in focus.
- It is advisable to
  (a) have a spare bulb for the projector
  (b) run through the slide programme to ensure that all the slides are in the correct order, the right way up and the right way round!

Session

1. Welcome and prayer

- The catechists welcome everyone.
- Using the handout on p. 35, introduce and say the prayer together. This handout should be in the candidates' files, though it may be advisable to have a few spare copies available!

> ... pour out your Spirit
> upon your people,
> and grant us
> a new vision of your glory,
> a new experience of your power,
> a new faithfulness to your Word,

Welcome the Spirit

    a new consecration to your service,
    that your love may grow among us,
    and your kingdom come;
    through Christ, our Lord.
    Amen.

- Collect the handout on pp. 56–57, 'I Have Called You by Name'. (The chosen names for Confirmation should be entered on the Confirmation cards.)

2. Reflection on the Celebration of Election

- The catechist reflects with the candidates on the Celebration of Election inviting them to share their thoughts and feelings about the celebration:
  — Did you enjoy the Celebration?
  — Was this an important thing to do?
  — Why was it important?

3. Presentation and activities I

- The catechist introduces the Unit, which is about celebrating. Ask the candidates what the word 'celebrating' means to them, and if they can remember any celebrations which were especially memorable.

- Distribute the handout on pp. 123–124 *or* the one on p. 125. ('Celebrating', on p. 125, may be more suitable for older candidates.) Ask the candidates to complete it either individually or in pairs. Having given time for this activity, the catechist should list on a large sheet of paper the items which the candidates have identified.

- If using the handout on pp. 123–124 give out the handouts on pp. 126–130.
  (*N.B. each pair of candidates is asked to complete only one of these handouts.*)

- When one or both of these exercises are completed the catechist should draw together the responses and summarize them.
  (*N.B. the catechist may need to add ideas so that the summary includes the following*):
  (a) we celebrate because something important is happening in our lives
  (b) we celebrate people and events which are important
  (c) we celebrate to let people know that we love and care about them
  (d) we celebrate in order to feel close to each other and to feel part of a group or community.

- The catechist, drawing on personal experience, explains that very often families or groups develop their own particular ways of celebrating, for instance:
  — At Christmas, in our family, we always go to Midnight Mass and when we come home we have bacon sandwiches
  — In our family we always hang our stockings by the fire
  — In our family we always have dinner . . .
  — In our family we always have our presents . . .

- Discuss with the candidates whether they have any particular traditions in their family.

- The catechist now explains that in the Church we celebrate various important events and that over the centuries the family of the Church has developed its own special way of celebrating.

4. Refreshment break
5. Presentation and activities II

- The Rite of Confirmation is now explained, using the slide–tape presentation, the text of which is given here:

Slide 1   Confirmation Day—a great day for young people from various parishes in the area, who gather with their families, sponsors and fellow parishioners to celebrate the great Sacrament of Confirmation. Over the past few months they have been preparing for this day when, in a special way, the Holy Spirit will be given to strengthen them to live as Christians in the world of today.

Slide 2   Everyone stands as the Bishop, wearing his mitre and carrying his crozier, enters in procession. As leader of the local church and as a successor of the Apostles, to whom the Holy Spirit was first given, he will celebrate the Sacrament. He will give, in the name of God and the Church, the gift which Jesus promised would be sent.

Slide 3   The Mass has begun—the most important celebration in the lives of Catholics. In it we unite ourselves with Jesus and each other and renew our commitment to bring the message of love into the world.

Slide 4   After the greeting and the opening prayers we listen to the scriptures. The readings at the Confirmation Mass remind us of Jesus' promise that the Holy Spirit would be sent in power to strengthen and help his followers. This promise will be fulfilled in the lives of the young people who will be presented to the Bishop.

Slide 5   After the readings and the Bishop's homily, those who are to be confirmed are asked to stand and renew their baptismal promises. The Bishop asks them to declare their choice for Jesus in front of the whole congregation. He first asks them if they reject sin and promise to fight against evil, then he asks them to state openly that they believe in God the Creator, in Jesus the Lord and in the Holy Spirit.

Slide 6   Once this great statement of belief is made the Bishop prays for those to be confirmed. Extending his arms, a symbol of calling down God's power, the Bishop prays that they will be filled with the Holy Spirit and receive the seven gifts which were promised.

Slide 7   The Confirmation candidates are now brought forward to the Bishop by their sponsors. The sponsors represent the whole community which wants these young men and women to receive the gift of the Holy Spirit.

Slide 8   The Bishop now confers the Sacrament. Placing his hand on the head of each candidate, calling down God's power, he anoints each one with oil, called chrism, tracing the sign of the Cross on the person's forehead. The oil represents strength—the strength which will be needed to live as true followers of Jesus. This signing with the Cross represents that we are marked with God's sign. As the Bishop does this he says the person's name and adds 'be sealed with the gift of the Holy Spirit'. The candidate answers 'Amen'.

Slide 9   The Bishop now greets the newly confirmed with the words 'Peace be with you'. The newly confirmed reply 'And also with you'. To live as a follower of Jesus may not always be easy but it will bring us a deep peace and contentment.

Welcome the Spirit

Slide 10 When all the candidates have been confirmed, the Bishop leads the congregation in special prayers for the newly confirmed, for their families and friends, for the Church and for the whole world.

Slide 11 The Mass continues. Some of the newly confirmed bring the gifts of bread and wine to the Bishop, which, at the Consecration, become the Body and Blood of Jesus Christ. Gathered round the Lord's table, the community once more is united to Jesus in offering praise and thanks to God.

Slide 12 When we receive the Body and Blood of Jesus Christ we deepen our friendship with him and find the strength to live each day with him and for him. Through this sharing we are united with each other and together we are called to work for God.

Slide 13 The Confirmation Celebration ends with a special blessing. The newly confirmed are sent out to spread the Good News and to live in a special way as followers of Jesus, bringing joy, peace and friendship into the lives of others . . .

Slide 14 at home . . .

Slide 15 with friends . . .

Slide 16 in all the world.

- If it is not possible to use the slides and tape, the catechist should explain the structure of the Rite of Confirmation and give simple explanations for each part of it:

(a) *The Gathering* – emphasize the idea of the whole community sharing in the joy of this special occasion.

(b) *The Entry of the Bishop* – stress the link with the Apostles, the role of the Bishop as leader of the diocesan church to which we belong.

(c) *The Opening Rite* – emphasize that normally Confirmation is celebrated during Mass, which is the most important celebration of the family of the Church.

(d) *Liturgy of the Word* – point out that the readings will remind us that what is happening today is a fulfilment of the promise to send the Holy Spirit to help us to live and work for the Kingdom of God.

(e) *Renewal of Baptismal Promises* – stress that because we are invited to draw closer to God we must reject all that is evil in our lives and accept Jesus as Lord of our lives.

(f) *Laying on of Hands* – explain that this symbolizes the calling down of God's power and strength.

(g) *Presentation of Candidates by their Sponsors* – highlight the importance of the sponsors, who represent the community which will support and help us to live as God wants. At this point the significance of the Confirmation name can be discussed, using the handout on pp. 56–57, 'I Have Called You by Name'.

(h) *The Chrismation* – recap on the significance of the four elements of the sacramental action as outlined in Unit Four:
— Laying on of hands
— Anointing with chrism
— Signing with the sign of the Cross.
— Words, 'N. be sealed . . .'

Unit Seven: Preparing to Celebrate

(i) *Greeting of Peace* – point out that when we respond to God we are promised the gift of peace, no matter what difficulties we may face.

(j) *Prayers of the Faithful* – explain these are the ways in which the community prays for us and our needs.

(k) *Liturgy of the Eucharist* – emphasize that because Confirmation calls us to be witnesses and workers for the Kingdom of God we need constantly to renew our strength for the task given to us. Sharing in the Eucharist is the way in which we can find this strength.

(l) *Communion Rite* – through Communion we strengthen and deepen our relationship with Jesus and with one another. Receiving Communion under the form of bread and wine is now encouraged as a sign of that union.

(m) *Blessing* – point out that a special blessing prayer is used.

- Distribute the handout on p. 131, 'Put It in Order' (make sure the cards are well shuffled) and ask the candidates to arrange the cards marked 'A' in their correct sequence and then match them with the cards marked 'B'.

6. Prayer

- Hymn: Sing the first verse of 'Come Holy Ghost, Creator Come'.
- Litany:
  (The leader announces the response: 'Come, Holy Spirit, come.')

    Loving God, we ask that your Spirit will come in power to us as we say:
    R/ Come, Holy Spirit, come.
    Spirit of truth, teach us your ways, as we say:
    R/ Come, Holy Spirit, come.
    Spirit of love, help us to serve, as we say:
    R/ Come, Holy Spirit, come.
    Spirit of courage, give us your strength, as we say:
    R/ Come, Holy Spirit, come.
    Spirit of peace, live within us, as we say:
    R/ Come, Holy Spirit, come.
    Spirit of joy, fill our hearts, as we say:
    R/ Come, Holy Spirit, come.

- Bidding Prayers:

    Spirit of God, teach us to pray. We bring before you, loving God, ourselves, our families and our friends. We ask you to bless us all and keep us in your care. Lord, hear us ...

Now invite the candidates to name anyone or any intention they wish the group to pray for ... (pause)

Let us now pray to God the Father in the words Jesus taught us:
Our Father ...

- Blessing by catechist:

    Go forth into the world in peace.
    Be of good courage;
    hold fast to that which is good;
    render to no one evil for evil;
    strengthen the faint-hearted;
    support the weak;
    help the afflicted;
    honour all people.
    Love and serve the Lord,
    rejoicing in the power of the Holy Spirit,
    and the blessing of God Almighty,
    the Father, the Son and the Holy Spirit,
    be upon us and remain with us always.
    Amen.

- Hymn: Last two verses of 'Come, Holy Ghost'.

7. Conclusion

- The catechist should explain the Celebration of Sending Forth and give details of the time and place, etc.
- The catechist should now outline the practical details for the Confirmation Day, e.g. time, place, date, seating arrangements, etc.
- Ensure that the Confirmation cards have been completed.
- Distribute the prayer leaflet, the handout on pp. 132–133, 'A Day at a Time', which should be photocopied on two sides of A4 and folded into three.
- Thank the candidates for coming.

Team reflection

1. Did the session go well? Make a note of any adaptations you would recommend for future use.
2. Were there any reflections on the Celebration of Election worth noting?
3. Have any problems emerged? How can they be dealt with?

CELEBRATING – WHAT MAKES A CELEBRATION? (e.g. Music, Singing)

Birthday

_____

_____

_____

_____

_____

_____

_____

_____

Christmas

_____

_____

_____

_____

Football Win

© Sister Mary Bernard Potter SP and Nigel Bavidge 1993.
Multiple copies of this page may be made by the purchasing church or group only.

WHAT MAKES A CELEBRATION? (CONTINUED)

Wedding

_____

_____

_____

_____

_____

First Communion

_____

_____

_____

_____

_____

© Sister Mary Bernard Potter SP and Nigel Bavidge 1993.
Multiple copies of this page may be made by the purchasing church or group only.

PREPARING TO CELEBRATE

CELEBRATING

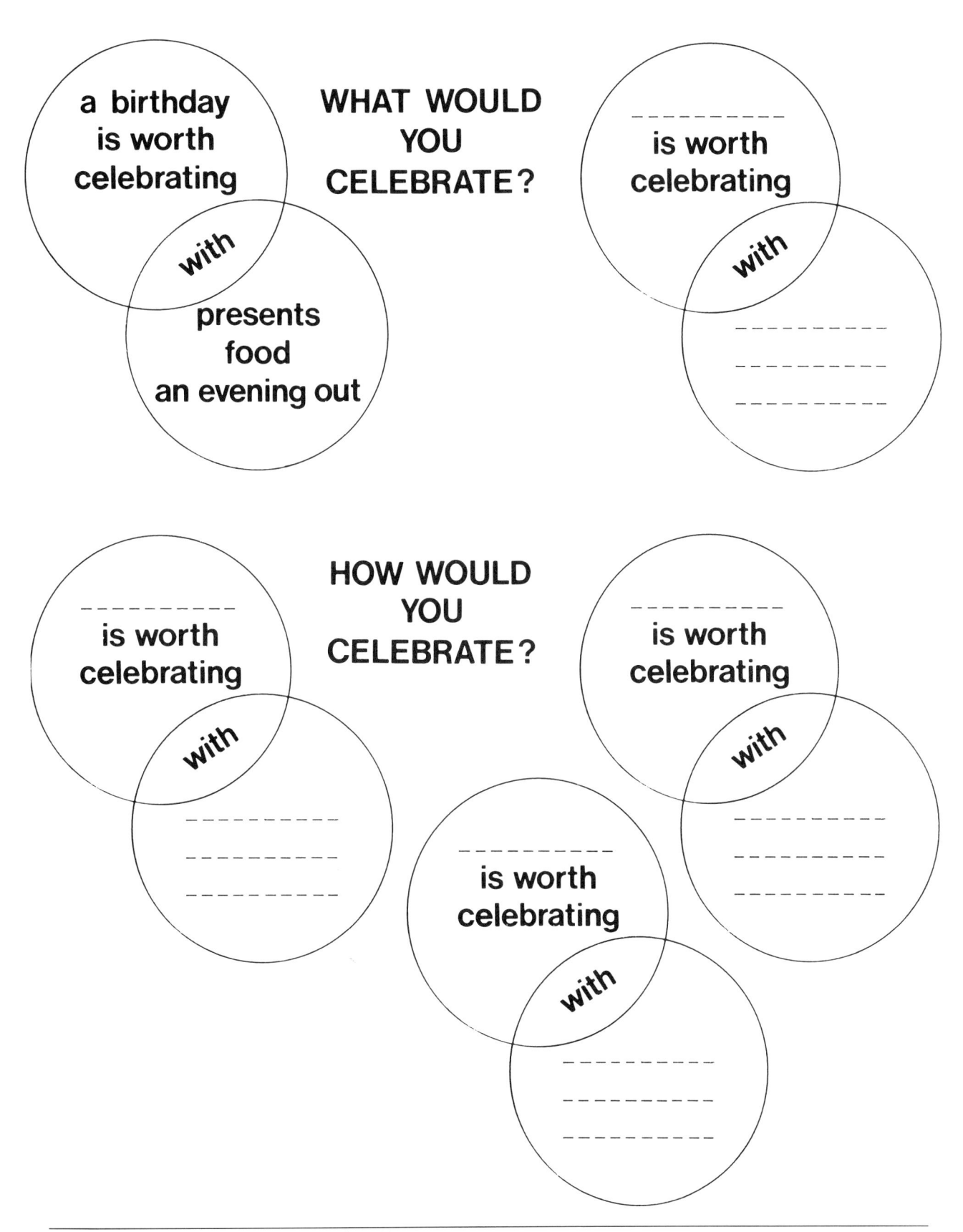

a birthday is worth celebrating **with** **presents food an evening out**

WHAT WOULD YOU CELEBRATE?

---------- **is worth celebrating** **with** ---------- ---------- ----------

HOW WOULD YOU CELEBRATE?

---------- **is worth celebrating** **with** ---------- ---------- ----------

---------- **is worth celebrating** **with** ---------- ---------- ----------

---------- **is worth celebrating** **with** ---------- ---------- ----------

© Sister Mary Bernard Potter SP and Nigel Bavidge 1993.
Multiple copies of this page may be made by the purchasing church or group only.

PREPARING TO CELEBRATE

CELEBRATING CHRISTMAS

Why do people celebrate Christmas?

1. _____

2. _____

3. _____

4. _____

5. _____

Now put your reasons in order of importance. For example, if you think your third reason is most important put No. 3 in Box A and so on.

A	B	C	D	E

© Sister Mary Bernard Potter SP and Nigel Bavidge 1993.
Multiple copies of this page may be made by the purchasing church or group only.

PREPARING TO CELEBRATE

CELEBRATING BIRTHDAYS

Why do people celebrate birthdays?

1. _____

2. _____

3. _____

4. _____

5. _____

Now put your reasons in order of importance. For example, if you think your third reason is most important put No. 3 in Box A and so on.

A	B	C	D	E

© Sister Mary Bernard Potter SP and Nigel Bavidge 1993.
Multiple copies of this page may be made by the purchasing church or group only.

PREPARING TO CELEBRATE

CELEBRATING FIRST COMMUNION

Why do people celebrate First Communion?

1. _____

2. _____

3. _____

4. _____

5. _____

Now put your reasons in order of importance. For example, if you think your third reason is most important put No. 3 in Box A and so on.

A	B	C	D	E

© Sister Mary Bernard Potter SP and Nigel Bavidge 1993.
Multiple copies of this page may be made by the purchasing church or group only.

PREPARING TO CELEBRATE

Celebrating a Wedding

Why do people celebrate a wedding?

1. _____

2. _____

3. _____

4. _____

5. _____

Now put your reasons in order of importance. For example, if you think your third reason is most important put No. 3 in Box A and so on.

A	B	C	D	E

© Sister Mary Bernard Potter sp and Nigel Bavidge 1993.
Multiple copies of this page may be made by the purchasing church or group only.

PREPARING TO CELEBRATE

CELEBRATING A FOOTBALL WIN

Why do people celebrate a football win?

1. _____

2. _____

3. _____

4. _____

5. _____

Now put your reasons in order of importance. For example, if you think your third reason is most important put No. 3 in Box A and so on.

A	B	C	D	E

© Sister Mary Bernard Potter SP and Nigel Bavidge 1993.
Multiple copies of this page may be made by the purchasing church or group only.

PREPARING TO CELEBRATE

PUT IT IN ORDER

Cut these boxes out.

A	B
A: THE GATHERING	**B:** Where you meet together in my name I am there
A: ENTRY OF BISHOP	**B:** We greet the Apostles' successor
A: THE OPENING RITE	**B:** The Bishop welcomes us to the celebration
A: LITURGY OF THE WORD	**B:** We listen to the Scriptures
A: RENEWAL OF BAPTISMAL PROMISES	**B:** We proclaim our Faith
A: LAYING ON OF HANDS	**B:** We pray that the Spirit will come to us
A: PRESENTATION OF CANDIDATES BY SPONSORS	**B:** Representatives of the community bring us forward
A: THE CHRISMATION	**B:** The Gift of the Holy Spirit is given
A: THE GREETING OF PEACE	**B:** My peace I leave you
A: PRAYERS OF THE FAITHFUL	**B:** We pray for each other
A: LITURGY OF THE EUCHARIST	**B:** Do this in memory of me
A: COMMUNION RITE	**B:** Take and eat; take and drink
A: BLESSING	**B:** Go in my name

© Sister Mary Bernard Potter SP and Nigel Bavidge 1993.
Multiple copies of this page may be made by the purchasing church or group only.

DAY THREE

Holy Spirit of God
be with me as I prepare for my
 Confirmation tomorrow.
May it be a special day
for me,
for my family,
for my friends
and for all the parish.

Holy Spirit of love
I thank you for all those who have
 helped me
to prepare for Confirmation.
Bless . . . (name people at home
 you want God to bless),
bless them for all they have done for me.
I ask you to bless all those in my
 Confirmation group,
especially . . . (name any members
 of the group you want to pray for).

Holy Spirit of strength
come to me in power
and help me to live like Jesus.
Give me a generous heart
so that I may be kind and caring.
Give me a brave heart
so that I may always do what is right.
Give me a loyal heart
so that I may always be
a true follower of Jesus.

Day by day, . . .

Glory be to the Father . . .

CONFIRMATION DAY

Loving God
may your Spirit come
to me this day.
May your Spirit come
with power.
May your Spirit help
me to live
in joy,
in peace,
in love.
May your Spirit
give me courage,
strength and power
to live as you want.
This prayer I make in
Jesus' name.
 Amen.

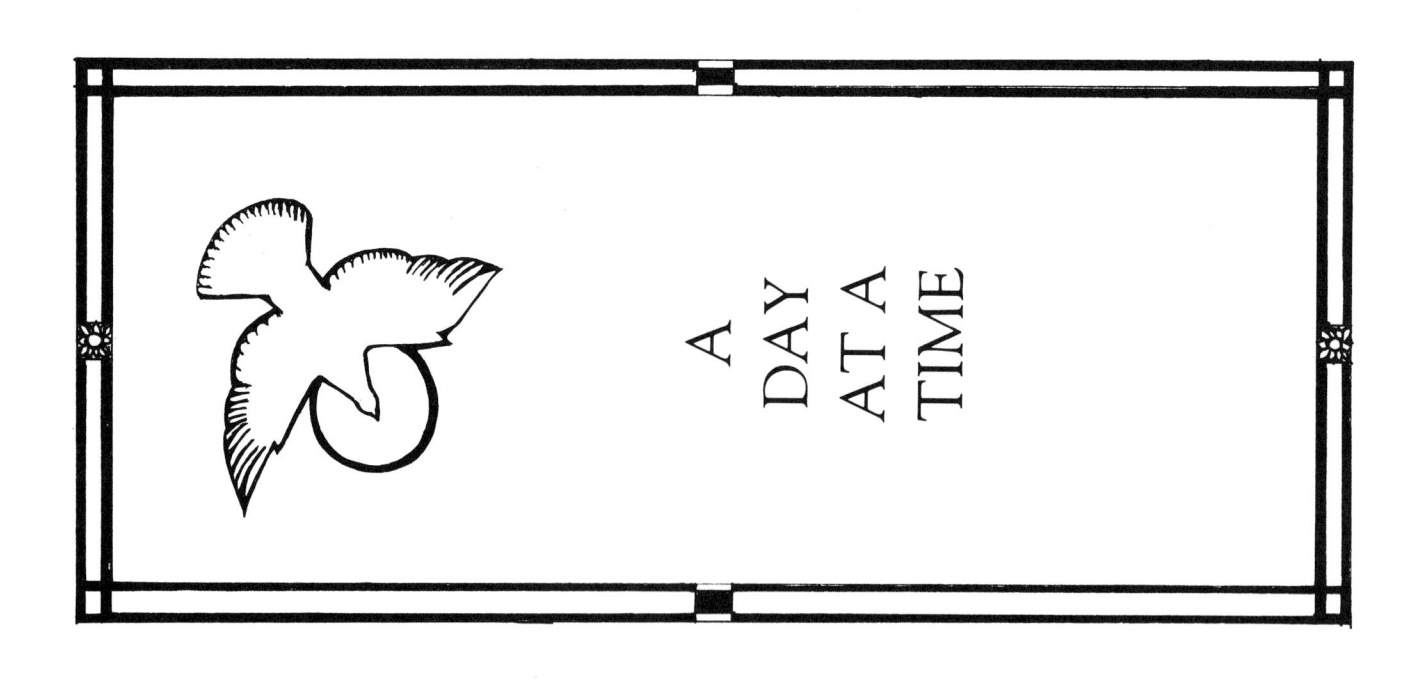

A DAY AT A TIME

© Sister Mary Bernard Potter SP and Nigel Bavidge 1993.
Multiple copies of these pages may be made by the purchasing church or group only.

Confirmation Day is nearly here and in order to be ready it is important to *pray*.

Jesus promised that our prayers would always be heard and that God will always give us what is good for us.

Here are some prayers for you to say. There is a prayer for each of the three days leading up to your Confirmation Day.

DAY ONE

Loving God,
I thank you for creating me.
I thank you for my life
and all the good things which happen to me.
I thank you especially for . . .
    (think of some special people and special
    times in your life).

I thank you for Jesus, your Son,
who came to show us how to live in joy and peace.

I know that it will not always be easy
to live as Jesus taught us
and so, my God, I ask you to send me
the Holy Spirit
to give me strength
to always be loyal and true.

Day by day,
three things I pray,
to see you more clearly,
love you more dearly,
and to follow you more nearly.

Glory be to the Father and to the Son
    and to the Holy Spirit,
as it was in the beginning,
    is now, and ever shall be,
world without end.
Amen.

DAY TWO

Lord Jesus,
you came among us
to show us how to live.

You died on the cross
to tell us how much you love us.
You rose from the dead in glory
for you are God's Son.

You sent your Spirit to live in our hearts
so that your love
can be in our world today.

Help me to be kind and loving to all.
Help me to serve others as you did.
Help me to forgive anyone who hurts me.

Help me to follow you always
and find the peace and joy
which you promised.

Day by day,
three things I pray,
to see you more clearly,
love you more dearly,
and to follow you more nearly.

Glory be to the Father and to the Son
    and to the Holy Spirit,
as it was in the beginning,
    is now, and ever shall be,
world without end.
Amen.

Celebration of Sending Forth

Celebration Aims

This celebration is an important part of the preparation of the Confirmation candidates.

Its purposes are:
1. To re-emphasize for the candidates the importance of the Sacrament.

2. To highlight the community joy in presenting its young members for Confirmation.

3. To recognize the community's involvement in the sacramental development of its young people.

4. To emphasize the relationship between the parish and the diocese.

Outline

This celebration should take place just before the final blessing during one particular Sunday Eucharist in the parish or at the Sunday Eucharist which the candidates normally attend on the Sunday immediately preceding the Celebration of the Sacrament of Confirmation.

A sample text for the Celebration is given in this section and on the handout on pp. 137–138. It is suggested that the name of the parish and the date of the Celebration of Sending Forth should be added to the front of the cover, and the names of the candidates to the back of the cover, before photocopying.

STRUCTURE

- Invitation
- Prayer
- Sending forth
- Blessing and dismissal

MATERIALS

- Copies of the Celebration of Sending Forth for everyone.

THE CELEBRATION OF SENDING FORTH OF CANDIDATES FOR THE SACRAMENT OF CONFIRMATION

Invitation

Priest: On (day of Confirmation), our Bishop will celebrate the Sacrament of Confirmation. Over the past few months (weeks) some of our young people have been preparing for this great day.

       I now invite them to come forward.

Prayer

When the candidates have come to the sanctuary, the priest extends his hands over them and prays:

Priest: God of love,
    we praise and thank you
    for these, our brothers and sisters,
    who ask for the Sacrament of Confirmation.
    We ask you to pour out your Spirit upon them
    and fill them with your gifts
    in the name of Jesus Christ, our Lord.

All: Amen.

Sending Forth

Priest: In the name of God, our Creator,
    in the name of Jesus, our Saviour,
    in the name of the life-giving Spirit,
    and in the name of this our parish,
    we are proud to present you to our Bishop.
    Go now from this Mass with God's blessing
    and with the prayers of this community
    to be sealed with the gift of the Holy Spirit.

Blessing and Dismissal

Priest: May Almighty God bless you all . . .

       The Mass is ended, go in the peace of Christ.

All: Amen.

Celebration of Sending forth of candidates for confirmation

Parish of _____

Date _____

CANDIDATES' NAMES

© Sister Mary Bernard Potter sp and Nigel Bavidge 1993.
Multiple copies of these pages may be made by the purchasing church or group only.

This Celebration of Sending Forth is an important part of the parish preparation of the candidates for the Sacrament of Confirmation.

The purposes of the Celebration are:

- to re-emphasize for the candidates the importance of the sacrament
- to highlight the community's joy in presenting its young members for Confirmation
- to recognize the community's involvement in the sacramental development of its young people
- to emphasize the relationship between the parish and the diocese.

CELEBRATION OF SENDING FORTH

Invitation

Priest: On (day of Confirmation), our Bishop will celebrate the Sacrament of Confirmation. Over the past few months (weeks) some of our young people have been preparing for this great day.

I now invite them to come forward.

Prayer

When the candidates have come to the sanctuary, the priest extends his hands over them and prays:

Priest: God of love,
we praise and thank you
for these, our brothers and sisters,
who ask for the Sacrament of Confirmation.
We ask you to pour out your Spirit upon them
and fill them with your gifts
in the name of Jesus Christ, our Lord.

All: Amen.

Sending Forth

Priest: In the name of God, our Creator,
in the name of Jesus, our Saviour,
in the name of the life-giving Spirit,
and in the name of this our parish,
we are proud to present you to our Bishop.
Go now from this Mass with God's blessing
and with the prayers of this community
to be sealed with the gift of the Holy Spirit.

Blessing and Dismissal

Priest: May Almighty God bless you all . . .

The Mass is ended, go in the peace of Christ.

All: Amen.

Unit 8

INTO THE FUTURE

UNIT AIMS

1. To give the newly confirmed the opportunity to *reflect* on the Celebration of the Sacrament and its application for their lives.

2. To emphasize that the gift of Confirmation brings responsibilities which we are enabled to fulfil through the power of the Spirit working within us.

3. To celebrate spiritually and socially the experience of the preparation for and the reception of the Sacrament of Confirmation.

OUTLINE

1. Welcome and prayer
2. Presentation and activities
3. Refreshments
4. Closing hymn

MATERIALS

'Prayer' (handout on p. 142)
'What I Thought' (handout on p. 143)
'Fruits of the Spirit' (handout on p. 144)
'A Call to Action' (handout on p. 145)
'When You Do These Things' (handout on p. 146)

'What Do I Do Now, Lord?' (handout on p. 147)
Felt-tip pens, pencils and pens
Large sheets of paper
Hymn books

Welcome the Spirit

PREPARATION

- Create a party atmosphere in the room.
- Refreshments—these should be special in order to emphasize the sense of celebration.
- Tape recorder and quiet music, if used.

SESSION

1. Welcome and prayer

- The catechists welcome everyone.
- Introduce (see the handout on p. 142) and say together the prayer.

   …, you have poured out your Spirit
   upon us in a special way.
   Continue to pour out your Spirit
   upon your people,
   and grant us
   a new vision of your glory,
   a new experience of your power,
   a new faithfulness to your Word,
   a new consecration to your service,
   that your love may grow among us,
   and your kingdom come;
   through Christ, our Lord.
   Amen.

2. Presentation and activities

- The catechist leads a discussion on:
   (a) the experiences of the celebration of the Sacrament of Confirmation,
   (b) the feelings of the newly confirmed about the whole of the preparation process.
   (*N.B. It is vital for the future development of Confirmation catechesis and celebration that the catechist should make careful note of what the newly confirmed have to say.*)

- After the discussion distribute the handout on p. 143, 'What I Thought', and ask the newly confirmed to complete it. Explain that these completed handouts will be collected and the information used for future planning of Confirmation preparation. Collect the completed handouts.

- Introduce the next section by reminding the newly confirmed that Confirmation is a vocation (call from God) to live more fully as disciples of Jesus in their everyday lives by loving and serving others in the name of Jesus (mission).

- Remind the newly confirmed that through the Sacrament of Confirmation they have been given the seven gifts of the Holy Spirit and if they use these gifts their lives, like the lives of other Christians, will show special qualities which we call 'the fruits of the Spirit'.

- Ask the newly confirmed to name the qualities which should be evident in the lives of followers of Jesus. List these qualities on large sheets of paper.

- Using the handout on p. 144, 'Fruits of the Spirit', ask the newly confirmed to put these qualities under the appropriate headings.

- Explain that Jesus gave us a plan of action for these fruits to grow. Distribute the handout on p. 145, 'A Call to Action', and read through this Gospel passage with the newly confirmed.

- Then, using the phrase 'When I was hungry, you gave me food', draw out from the newly confirmed the kinds of hunger experienced by different people, and the kinds of 'food' that can be offered, e.g.:
  — Hunger of the body – contributing to aid programmes, famine areas
  — Hunger of the mind – desire for education (Third World)
  — Hunger of the heart – love and friendship
  — Hunger of the spirit – a reason for living.

- Having worked through this one phrase with the group, distribute the handout on p. 146, 'When You Do These Things', for completion. When this activity is finished draw together the various responses.

- At the end of this discussion, distribute the handout on p. 147, 'What Do I Do Now, Lord?'. Invite the group to sit quietly to reflect on these words as you slowly read them through. It would be a good idea to play some quiet music while you do this. Allow plenty of time for this reflection. Explain that this reflection is personal and that they will not be asked to share their thoughts or ideas.

- The catechist should bring this section to a close by thanking the members of the group for their friendship, loyalty and commitment.

3. Refreshments

The refreshments offered for this last session should be special to emphasize the sense of joy and celebration.

4. Closing hymn

Just before the ending of the session, gather the group into a circle and sing some suitable hymn together, e.g.

'Bind Us Together, Lord'
'Our God Reigns'
'Let There Be Love'.

Team reflection

1. Did the session go well? Make a note of any adaptations you would recommend for future use.

2. Have any problems emerged? How can they be dealt with?

SESSION PRAYER

Our prayer now is changed. God has sent the Holy Spirit to you, just as Jesus promised. We ask God to fill us with love through the power of the Holy Spirit.

... you have poured out your Spirit
upon us in a special way.
Continue to pour out your Spirit
upon your people,
and grant us
a new vision of your glory,
a new experience of your power,
a new faithfulness to your word,
a new consecration to your service,
that your love may grow among us,
and your kingdom come;
through Christ, our Lord.
Amen.

© Sister Mary Bernard Potter SP and Nigel Bavidge 1993.
Multiple copies of this page may be made by the purchasing church or group only.

INTO THE FUTURE

WHAT I THOUGHT

A. **What did you feel about the Confirmation celebration?**

1. Was it impressive? *Yes/No*

2. Did you feel part of the celebration? *Yes/No*

3. Were the hymns suitable? *Yes/No*

4. List here any suggestions for improving the celebration.

B. **What have you felt about the Confirmation Preparation Programme?**

1. Have you enjoyed the Programme? *Yes/No/OK*

2. Has the preparation been *too long/too short/about right?*

3. Did you find the work *difficult/easy/about right?*

4. List here any suggestions for improving the Preparation Programme.

C. **A friend of yours wants to be confirmed next year and asks you what you felt about the Confirmation Programme.**

What would you say?

© Sister Mary Bernard Potter SP and Nigel Bavidge 1993.
Multiple copies of this page may be made by the purchasing church or group only.

INTO THE FUTURE

FRUITS OF THE SPIRIT

Jesus says:

'I have called you to bear much fruit.'

Fruits shown on a bunch of grapes: Charity, Joy, Patience, Long Suffering, Peace, Goodness, Gentleness, Kindness, Self Control, Truthfulness, Faith, Right Loving

© Sister Mary Bernard Potter SP and Nigel Bavidge 1993.
Multiple copies of this page may be made by the purchasing church or group only.

A CALL TO ACTION

This is a reading from the Gospel of Matthew (Chapter 25)

Jesus said to his disciples,

When the King comes in glory,
he will sit on his throne with all his angels around him.
All the people of the world will come to him,
and he will separate them
just as a shepherd separates the sheep from the goats.
Then the King will say to the sheep,

'Come and receive your share of the kingdom
which I have prepared for you.
For when I was hungry, you gave me food.
When I was thirsty, you gave me a drink.
When I was a stranger, you made me feel welcome.
When I had nothing to wear, you gave me clothes.
When I was sick you took care of me,
and when I was in prison you came and visited me.'

The people who hear these words will ask,

'When did we see you hungry and give you food?
When did we see you thirsty and give you a drink?
When did we take you in and make you feel welcome?
When did we give you clothes to wear?
When did we see you sick or in prison and come to visit you?'

And the King will answer,

'When you do those things
for any of my brothers and sisters in need, you do it for me.
And those who do these things will live with God forever.'

This is the Good News of the Lord.

© Sister Mary Bernard Potter SP and Nigel Bavidge 1993.
Multiple copies of this page may be made by the purchasing church or group only.

INTO THE FUTURE

'When you do these things'

> 'When I was thirsty, you gave me a drink.
> When I was a stranger, you made me feel welcome.
> When I had nothing to wear, you gave me clothes.
> When I was sick, you took care of me,
> and when I was in prison, you came and visited me.'

Choose **one** of these lines and make a list of the ways in which people can be thirsty, a stranger, have nothing to wear, or be sick or in prison.

Think not only of the obvious ways in which people experience these things, but think of ways in which the people you know might experience them.

For example, an elderly person may be 'in prison' because they cannot get out of their own homes, or someone at school may be 'thirsty' for a friend.

List the ways in which you can help them.

Which line are you choosing?

'When I was _____,'

List of Needs   **List of Helps**

_____   _____
_____   _____
_____   _____
_____   _____
_____   _____
_____   _____
_____   _____
_____   _____

© Sister Mary Bernard Potter SP and Nigel Bavidge 1993.
Multiple copies of this page may be made by the purchasing church or group only.

INTO THE FUTURE

'WHAT DO I DO NOW, LORD?'

You are a special person . . . God gives you life . . .

God loves you . . .

Within you lives the Spirit of love who calls you to bring life and love to others . . .

Be still, . . .

    Listen to God who is calling to you now . . .

        to *love* . . .

Be still, . . .

What do I do now, Lord? . . .

How can I bring the Spirit of Love
into my home? . . .

into my school? . . .

to my friends? . . .

to the needy world? . . .

(*You may like to write down your thoughts.*)

© Sister Mary Bernard Potter SP and Nigel Bavidge 1993.
Multiple copies of this page may be made by the purchasing church or group only.